I Think I've Done Pretty Good!

Ruby Mae (Etherton) Owens
Her Life, Her Family

Nancy,
I enjoy seeing and
talking with you every
6 months or so.

Jim O.

JAMES M. OWENS

Lulu Publishing Services rev. date: 6/4/2014

Contents

Introduction vii

Chapter 1   Life on the Farm 1

Chapter 2   High School and College 19

Chapter 3   Teaching in One Room Schools, Marriage 23

Chapter 4   Living in Chicago, The Bomber Plant, First Child 33

Chapter 5   Living in Romulus, 2nd Child, Father's Death 43

Chapter 6   Life on Farnum Street, The Third Child. 51

Chapter 7   Death of Husband 67

Chapter 8   Family Deaths 77

Chapter 9   The Last of a Generation 83

Introduction

For the past several years, I have tried to have lunch with my mother, Ruby Mae (Etherton) Owens, once a week. My sisters, Judy and Jane, fortunately see her more often. Mother is the last of her generation on both sides of the family. She is one of the oldest individuals I have ever known, currently ninety-seven years of age. Clearly she values and takes pleasure in talking about her past.

Through the years, she has shared numerous interesting stories of her past. Her childhood experiences were so drastically different from those of my generation, let alone those of subsequent generations. She, of course, will not be around forever. I wanted to know more about her life. I wanted to pass on to younger generations of our family and others what I learned.

In 2009, I began taking a pad of paper and a pen to our weekly lunches; sometimes I brought a tape recorder. We began talking about the early days: about life on the farm, her mother, her father, her brothers and sisters. I brought it to a close when she was 97 years of age, tracing her life from 1915 to 2012.

I suspect there will be some minor inaccuracies in this sketch. For the most part, I relied on my mother's memory and that of others; checking facts when I could and adding what I thought were notable details. I probably did not get everything completely correct. Be assured, no errors or inaccuracies were intentional.

I had a lot of help. Many relatives contributed, especially my two sisters Judy and Jane. There are a number of friends who read drafts, made corrections and suggestions. My wife Rochelle Balkam was my primary editor and supporter. She made numerous improvements in regard to form and direction of content.

I certainly gained a great deal through these conversations with my mother and my relatives. I hope you enjoy this sketch of life centered on Ruby Mae (Etherton) Owens, my mother, an exceptional woman.

I think she did pretty good!

1 *Life on the Farm*
Birth to age 14.

O n March 27, 1915, the fourth child of Sarah Ellen (Gibson) Etherton and Grover Jackson Etherton was born in Johnston City, Williamson County, Illinois. The couple named their child Ruby Mae. Sarah and Grover's first child, Jewel Lorena, died when she was just two weeks old. Ruby's surviving older siblings were named William Wayne and Opal Louise. William Wayne was almost always called Wayne. After Ruby's birth, Earl Nelson, Mary Lucille, Florence Lillian, and an unnamed child were born. The unnamed child died at birth. Ruby remembers that her parents sent the children fishing on that mournful day in 1921.

Sarah and Grover were born, raised, lived, and died in Southern Illinois. Grover spent his childhood in Williamson County just a few miles away from the farm Sarah and he purchased as a young married couple. Grover left the area only twice for any significant period of time until they sold the farm. The first time was during World War I, working for two years in the coalmines in Johnston City, Illinois. While there, Sarah gave birth to Ruby and younger brother Earl. They returned to their farm soon after Earl was born.

Grover contracted a serious case of flu during the great flu epidemic that swept the United States in the teen years of the 20th century while in Johnston City. A relative on Sarah's side of the family who lived in the neighboring town of Herrin nursed Grover back to good health. Ruby is not completely sure of this relative's name. It was probably Nora (Bush) Blaine, daughter of Ruby's Aunt Vinnie Bush. Ruby noted, "Papa often said he owed his life to this relative."

Grover left the area for the second time in the summer of 1929, just after Ruby completed eighth grade. He and Sarah spent the summer working in Detroit.

Sarah grew up on the banks of the Little Wabash River in Clay County, Illinois. Her childhood home was approximately seventy-five miles northeast of Williamson County. It was a two and a half to three day trip by wagon at the time Sarah and her family moved to Williamson in the early nineteen hundreds. Sarah was probably sixteen years of age. On the trip each morning, the family would throw their dirty clothes in large metal cream cans filled with soapy water. The soap was homemade. The clothes swished in the soapy mix all day as the wagons traveled over rough unpaved roads. The wet clean clothes were hung on tree branches and bushes to dry when the travelers stopped for the day.

The Etherton children always called their mother, Mom or Momma, and their father, Papa. The grandchildren called them Grandma and Papa. Grover gave his children nicknames: Wayne's was Man, Opal's - Woman, Ruby's - BeBe, Mary's - Douchy, Earl's - Boy, Florence's - Ponce.

Sarah and Grover purchased the farm on which they raised their children in 1910 or so, around the time Wayne was born. The couple borrowed the money needed to pay for the property from one of Grover's relatives, his sister Lily's husband, Hugh Miller. The loan and the 6% annual interest was paid off after the state of Illinois purchased the property for the Crab Orchard Recreational Area project in 1939.

The Etherton's hundred-acre farm was located approximately five miles east of Makanda, a quaint town in Williamson County, Illinois. Makanda was, and still is, a one street town at the bottom of two hills. At the time the family resided in the area, Makanda had a hardware, a dry-goods store, a variety store, a drug store, a clothing store, a blacksmith shop, a post office, and a railroad station. The variety store had a broad selection of goods, including farm tools, food, and even burial caskets. The drug store was owned by one of Grover's half brothers. The blacksmith shop's primary function was to repair farm equipment.

Ruby and Earl Etherton fall of 1917, Ruby is 2.5 years old

Five Etherton children, fall of 1919
Seated left to right: Earl, Mary, Ruby
Standing: Opal, Wayne

In the fall of 2008, Ruby and her daughters, Judy and Jane, visited the building that had been Uncle Doll's Makanda pharmacy. Ruby was surprised to find a five-inch by seven-inch picture with an image of her uncle hanging on a wall. A person working at the store was visibly delighted upon learning the identity of one of the men in this vintage photograph. The photograph has been displayed since the new owners acquired the building. The store still has the words "drug store" printed on one wall. Ruby suspects it is also left over from her uncle's time.

David Bennett was Uncle Doll's name. He was a licensed pharmacist, earning his degree in St. Louis. Ruby fondly recalls having her first ice cream sundae and her first taste of pineapple in Uncle Doll's store.

One or more members of Ruby's immediate family would travel to town at least once a week through most of the year, and three to four times a week when the crops were harvested. The family purchased very little from Makanda's stores. Regular purchases included sugar, twenty-four pound bags of flour, and lard. Other items that they could not raise or make were usually purchased from either Sears Roebuck or Montgomery Ward catalogs. The primary purpose for traveling to Makanda was to deliver their surplus vegetables, fruit, feathers, and milk products to the railroad station from which they were sent to markets in Chicago, Illinois.

Ruby has vivid memories of riding to town in a loaded mule drawn wagon. The mules were named Pearl and Old Jack, and they were less than cooperative at times. Many a trip was lengthened when this pair balked. When the mules decided to come to a stop, the only thing the passengers could do was to wait until the mules were ready to resume the trip. Ruby noted that Papa one time stabbed Old Jack with a knife in an attempt to get the mule to move. "Old Jack didn't move, he didn't care." Ruby said, "Old Jack did what he wanted to do." The contrary animal was clearly a model for the adage "stubborn as a mule." Grover eventually traded the old male mule to a neighboring farmer. One day, Old Jack jumped off a cliff and killed himself, Ruby recalls.

The farm was relatively small for this Southern Illinois area at the time. The property was within a mile from where the last great glacier stopped. As a result, the farm was very fertile but was rather hilly and the soil contained numerous troublesome rocks.

The Ethertons received mail by way of Makanda on a daily basis. The farm was located along rural route #2. Postage at the time was two cents per letter. The letter carrier delivered the mail in a horse drawn buggy. If you did not have stamps, you could leave the money in the mailbox, and the mailman would attach a stamp.

Most days on the farm were filled with an abundance of difficult labor. Ruby recalls spending day after day picking fruit, hoeing to control the ever-present weeds that competed with the crops, and doing other outdoor farming chores. There was little time for recreation. There was the occasional fishing trip, and Wayne went hunting frequently. These activities, of course, put food on the table. In the winter, when there was sufficient snow on the ground, the children enjoyed sledding down hills on the farm. Grover made wooden sleds for the children. He would round the wooden runners in front so that they would glide over the snow. Once the runners were carved, the children would use broken glass to smooth the wood surface to insure a fast trip down the hill. Ruby said it took a long time and a lot of scraping to sufficiently smooth the runners.

Ruby only remembers receiving one "store bought" toy as a child, a doll named Jenny. Earl was about two years old at the time and received an identical doll named Will. They were purchased by catalog, either Sears or Montgomery Wards. Sarah made a dress for Jenny and a little pair of overalls for Will.

Sarah strictly forbade cards in the house. She thought cards of any kind were sinful, the work of "Satan." Ruby recalls that she learned how to play solitaire while away at high school. Sarah found a deck of cards Ruby had brought home in the farmhouse and burned them.

The Ethertons did play checkers on occasion. They would draw a board onto cardboard with crayons and use corn for the pieces. One side used yellow corn and the other side used white corn. Ruby does not recall how they crowned kings.

A Shawnee Community College student interviewed Sarah in 1975. When asked: "What were some things that your family did for entertainment?" Ruby's mother responded: "They worked and when the day's work was done, they rested."

Picking blackberries was a major event in late summer each year. There were numerous blackberry bushes in the area, but chiggers were serious obstacles. Chiggers are tiny troublesome bugs that burrow under a person's skin and produce an aggravating itch that is extremely irritating. They are difficult to kill. If you live in an area where chiggers are known to exist, you learn to avoid places they are likely to be. A current day treatment for killing chiggers is to apply nail polish to the little red dot that appears on the affected person's skin that marks the entry of the chigger. It is believed that this will kill the irritating pest; the itch lingers for a couple of days regardless.

When the Etherton family went blackberry picking, they would dress in old, long, and heavy clothes. Even in temperatures in excess of 90 degrees, it was best to cover all parts of your body. Socks and rags were presoaked in kerosene and provided a chigger-barrier. When the picking for the day was complete, the workers would often jump into Falling Rock Creek to cool off and to remove the sweat, dirt, and kerosene. Falling Rock Creek was within a mile of the farm.

There was a small stand of tobacco on the farm, enough to supply Grover's and his mother-in-law's tobacco cravings. Sarah's mother, who occasionally stayed on the farm, often smoked tobacco in an old clay pipe. Grandma Gibson, as Ruby called her, rolled the tobacco leaves into a twist, making it convenient for her son-in-law to bite off a nice chunk or pull of tobacco. Grover constantly had a large pull of chewing tobacco in his mouth. Ruby recalls pulling weeds out of the tobacco patch, and recalls with disdain, pulling large green worms off the leaves and killing them. She remembers forcefully stomping on the worms to make sure they were dead. Ruby said, she "could not stand to touch those big green worms." The thought of the worms still makes her shiver.

Ruby's Grandma Gibson was particularly fond of a particular rocking chair at the farm. The children knew never to sit in the chair or touch the old "pocket book" that dangled from its back while their grandmother was present. Ruby remembers that the "pocket book" reeked of tobacco. The clay pipe and tobacco were stored in the purse when not in use. It smelled so bad that Ruby could not imagine touching the old "pocket book" anyway.

The house was in general disrepair. It had never been painted. All members of the family spent the majority of their time working the farm; little time was spent doing household duties. The two-story house consisted of a kitchen, a parlor, a living room, and two bedrooms. The parlor was used as a bedroom for some of the children, and the parents slept in the living room. Their toilet, which was common for this time in rural America, was outside.

In 1986, Eric Etherton's third grade class sought letters from grandparents. In response, Eric's grandfather and Ruby's younger brother Earl described the farmhouse. Earl noted, "My house was a small, two-story house which was never completely finished. It had no electricity and no plumbing. Part of the siding was gone and when it snowed in the winter, the snow would blow in on the covers."

In the early years on the farm, Grover built a cellar and Sarah, with the help of the children, filled it with canned goods each year. Ruby noted, "Mom would can anything." One time Wayne came home with forty rabbits from one of his hunting trips. Sarah canned the rabbit meat that they did not eat while fresh. The family would can peaches and molasses in gallon containers using bees-wax to seal the top. In addition to the cellar, the family preserved turnips and sweet potatoes by burying them in big holes lined with straw. Containers filled with cream and milk were suspended in a well or cistern to keep them cool.

The cellar was a big pit lined with rocks. The only access was a big wooden door. When needed, the cellar was used for storm protection. Ruby recalls retreating to the cellar several times a year. The family kept an ax in the cellar in case they got trapped and could not open the door. The ax was fortunately never used for this purpose.

There were several productive peach trees on the property, but the few apple trees on the property were rather disappointing. The strawberry plants were numerous and bountiful. The yield from the peach trees and strawberry plants were dependable sources of income.

There was a large variety of vegetables grown on the farm including tomatoes, corn, beans, cucumbers, asparagus, black-eyed peas, as well as sorghum cane to name a few. Asparagus was one of their best cash crops. There was consistently a hardy crop of black-eyed peas on the farm. Sarah would trade many of their black-eyed peas for navy beans in the neighboring town of Carterville.

Corn was planted by hand. Grover would plow and disk a field using their two mules, Pearl and Old Jack. Next, he would hook the mules up to a special small plow with which he would make perpendicular furrows. The children would then put two grains of corn in each point formed by the intersecting furrows. Grover then would cover the grain using a mule drawn machine called a harrow. The harrow had multiple steel teeth about ten inches in length, which smoothed and flattened the furrows and covered the grain.

The Ethertons raised their own popcorn. Ruby recalls that they would shuck the corn at the time it was harvested and store it. When they were ready to indulge, they would shell corn, remove the kernels from the cob, then place the kernels in a big black iron skillet and set it on top of a hot pot bellied stove. Once the corn had thoroughly popped, it was placed in a large dishpan and the family quickly consumed it. Ruby said they regarded it as a "real treat."

The entire family worked long hard hours in the fields during planting season. Ruby said what they did would be considered child abuse by today's standards. The Etherton children also planted corn at neighboring farms earning $1 per day for each worker. Sarah, Ruby noted, would take the bulk of their proceeds.

They would get very dirty working in fields each day. The children were barefoot most of the time when the weather permitted it. However, the Ethertons were typically too tired to bathe after spending so much of the day working. The children were required to wash their feet each evening. According to Ruby, they would average one bath per week. In between baths, they sponge bathed. Occasionally they would swim or bathe in nearby creeks. Most of the time they would fill a big metal washtub approximately two and a half feet in diameter with water. The entire family, six children and two adults, shared the same water. Ruby, in later years removed from the farm, really valued a long nice clean water bath in a modern porcelain tub.

The Ethertons typically each wore a set of clothes for a week. They would change clothes after they had their weekly bath, which usually occurred on the weekends.

When needed, Grover borrowed his brother's corn grinder to make corn meal for the family. The grinder was powered by a horse in a harness walking in a circle around the grinding apparatus. Corn bread, made from the corn meal, and milk were dinner staples.

Molasses was made from sorghum cane. Typically, Ruby and her siblings would peel the long leaves from the sorghum, and Grover would run the sorghum through a press placed over a big metal pan with a big handle. The resulting liquid, still in the pan, was placed over a big flaming pit positioned in a gully. The process would take at least a day, and Grover would need to stir the liquid almost constantly. When the hot liquid was deemed ready, it was pulled from the fire using the pan's big handle and left to cool. The end product was molasses.

There were some walnut trees along the side of a road near the farm. In the fall, once the walnuts had fallen from the trees, the family would hook up the two mules to the wagon and the entire family would travel to this stand of trees. They then filled the wagon bed with walnuts. The mules would pull the much heavier wagon back to the farm. The family would unload the wagon, putting the walnuts in piles. Next, they would take a baseball bat and beat the outside green skin or cover off the nuts. The process was called "hulling" the walnuts. The inner shells and nuts that were kept intact were sent to Chicago and sold.

The green skins, the hulls, turned brown after they were left outside for a few days. Sarah would put the hulls in a big old iron kettle filled with water placed over a fire in the yard. The water was brought to a boil. Then cloth was placed in the boiling brown mixture. When the cloth was pulled from the kettle, it was dyed brown. Brown did not show the dirt like white or light colored cloth.

Sarah made most of the families' clothing. Flour was one of the few things they purchased from stores, purchasing twenty-four pound sacks when needed. Once the flour was consumed, Sarah would rip apart the sacks at the seams, resulting in just about a square yard of nice white cloth. The flour sacks were dyed brown in the walnut hull mixture. They were then used to make many types of clothes.

Sarah made underwear for the entire family out of the dyed flour sacks. Ruby recalls one time a member of the family had a pair of homemade under-pants, which carried the label, " 100% pure" in the rear. She said: "The kids thought that was so funny." She thinks Wayne was probably the child that wore them. Of course, the "100% pure" label was advertising the purity of the flour.

The farm was also home to a varying number of chickens, geese, pigs, cattle, horses, and occasionally a goat or two. There were just enough pigs for personal meat consumption. They were not considered an income source. Typically, they had ten to twelve cows, usually Jerseys. Jersey cattle were preferred because of the quality and quantity of butter fat in their milk. According to Ruby, their milk contains better butter fat than that of other cattle. She recalls using a separator to divide the cattle's raw milk into cream and what was called "blue john." Butter was made from much of the cream. The blue john, so named because of its blue cast, was fed to the hogs. Cream was the farm's best selling product. It was delivered to the train station in Makanda and sent to markets in Chicago weekly.

There were also dogs and cats of varying numbers on this Southern Illinois farm. They were not considered pets. The dogs were used for hunting and cats for controlling the mice population. These animals were never allowed in the house except for a mouser, a cat that was good at catching mice.

Mattresses for the beds were homemade. Their beds had a lower mattress made of straw and a top mattress of feathers. The straw was harvested on the farm, and the feathers were plucked from the farm's geese. The fabric for the cloth, called ticking, which encased the straw and feathers, was purchased from Montgomery Wards catalogs. The feather ticks were made of a special fabric, which prevented the feathers from working their way out of the mattress. The straw ticks were of lesser quality and not as expensive.

Each early spring the geese would molt, shed their feathers. At this time of year, Sarah would catch one goose at a time, position it upside down between her legs, while sitting on a stool with Ruby holding the goose's feet and pluck the loose feathers. Sarah dressed in thick overhauls in order to prevent injury from the angry geese. The geese provided valuable down, some of which was used to make pillows and mattresses for personal use, but much of it was sent to markets in Chicago for the commercial production of down pillows. The down provided a reliable source of income.

One time a goose built a nest aside a corner fence post near the outhouse. Ruby remembers being chased by the protective mother on several occasions. Ruby says a goose bite really hurts.

11

Roosters would also chase the children when they were small. The roosters were faster than the young children. The skimpy underpants beneath the dresses that Sarah made for the girls provided little protection from the pecking pursuers. It was painful, Ruby recalls.

The few chickens on the farm were used for daily egg production and as a source of meat. When needed, Sarah would wring off the head of a chicken, pluck its feather, and prepare it for cooking. Chicken was usually served at the noon or evening meals, but occasionally, as a treat, the family would have fried chicken for breakfast. Each family member was assigned a particular part of the chicken to eat. Ruby got the wings.

Grover operated a steam-powered sawmill for material for the farm and as a source of income. The mill needed water to operate. Thus, it was always set up by a stream or creek. Sarah would typically fire-up and attend to the fire that transformed water into steam. Grover would feed logs to the mill producing usable boards of varying sizes.

Although Sarah in later years talked about how the drinking of alcohol was sinful, Grover had operated a still. Sarah, for that matter, would enjoy the occasional "toddy." "White Lightning" was yet another product the Ethertons traded or sold.

Bill Etherton, Wayne's only son, recalls a story passed down through Wayne. One time the family got word that the Ku Klux Klan was headed to the farm, possibly to destroy Grover's still. Sarah and the younger children were sent to a neighboring farm. Grover and Wayne spent the night in a ditch in wait, armed with guns. Fortunately, the KKK never appeared. Bill believes a neighbor intervened.

Paul M. Angel in his book, Bloody Williamson, describes how the KKK attempted to clean up Williamson County. He specifically noted how they hunted down stills and destroyed them.

The Ethertons purchased very little from stores. For the most part, they ate what they grew, made, raised, caught, killed, and butchered. This family was far from being rich. Ruby recalls frequently having only Southern Illinois corn bread and milk for dinner. There were no refrigerators or iceboxes. Food not canned was preserved in a cool well. Surplus crops, lumber, and milk products were sold anywhere they could find a buyer. The Chicago markets were the most reliable for the sale of produce, goose down, and cream. Peaches were usually peddled on streets in Carbondale, the largest town in the area, located about eight miles away.

Cooking was not something Sarah liked to do. She clearly preferred to work outside. Ruby became the primary family cook at a young age. A lot of the food was fried in lard. Each day there was a large breakfast usually consisting of eggs, bacon, and bread. Dinner was served around noon. They ate a lot of cornbread and milk supplemented with the vegetable and/or fruit of the season, chicken, beef, rabbit, squirrel, or canned goods. A dinner bell was rung to let family members know when the food was ready.

There was no electricity in the area at that time. At night the farmhouse was illuminated primarily with a kerosene lamp. The Ethertons owned three lamps but only used one at a time, wanting to conserve kerosene. The cleaning of the kerosene lamps was one of Ruby's jobs. She had hands small enough to fit into the lamp's glass chimney. It was not a job she enjoyed.

Another chore Ruby disliked was feeding and providing water for the mules. The troublesome Pearl, the female mule, often chased Ruby. Oddly, Ruby does not remember seeing the mule chase anyone else.

The clocks they had were unreliable. For the most part, the position of the sun was used to judge the time of day. Grover was especially good at telling the time from the sun.

Ruby, as a child and young adult, was plagued by what the family referred to as the "breaking-out." She remembers frequently breaking out in the morning and being exhausted by noon. Apparently Ruby suffered from some sort of allergy or multiple allergies. She would break out in hives, swell up, and itch all over. Grover once wrote Mayo Hospital but was not provided any useful information. He was told they could not do any thing without seeing Ruby in person at the hospital. Mayo was just too far away. One time, she was taken to a doctor in Herrin, a neighboring town about ten miles away. He was of no help. Ruby just learned to live with the suffering. The one useful thing the family discovered was that fish was one trigger to her "breaking-out."

The household had no running water or even hand pumps. Drinking water was obtained from a well with a bucket connected to a long chain. The chain was suspended from a big wheel that functioned as a pulley.

When the temperature fell below freezing, bare skin could stick to the chain. Sarah made mittens out of old clothes to avoid needless risk of injury.

There was an underground stream that fed the well. A creek ran through the farm, and Grover created a pond near the creek that served as a reservoir. The creek and adjacent pond provided water for the livestock. The muddy water was not suitable for human consumption.

During hot and dry summers, the well, creek, and pond would occasionally go dry. Grover was good at locating underground sources of water using a willow branch. This was called dousing. When needed, he would dig a hole and insert a tile from which the family would draw water from these alternate water sources.

Usually the alternate water sources were found on the property. One particularly dry summer, Ruby remembers Grover had to resort to a location off the property near Makanda. The water was transported back to the farm in fifty gallon barrels on mule drawn wagons.

Sarah was a devoted Missionary Baptist. She read the Bible regularly and assertively shared what she read with her family as well as anyone else who might be around. Sarah and the children went to church when they could. Grover went to church only on rare occasions. There were two churches in the area that they would attend. Neither had a full time minister. Services were only offered in the summer months when visiting ministers, circuit riders as they were called, passed through the area. Sarah's first choice was Pleasant Hill Baptist Church, which was just about a mile and a half from the farm. Liberty church was not a Baptist church but was in line with Sarah's firm beliefs. It was located about a mile a way. Both Pleasant Hill Baptist and Liberty had occasional family potluck dinners that the Ethertons, including Grover, enjoyed very much.

Ron Casmer, son of Florence, recalls a humorous story about his "grandma" regarding her religion. He and his wife, Bonnie, were taking Sarah back to her apartment after an outing. He noted, "The rain was so heavy, one could hardly see more than ten-fifteen feet (no kidding). I stopped the car and suggested to Grandma that we wait for the deluge to lighten up a bit. She exclaimed, 'Shoot! I'm a Baptist! I've been wet before!' And off she went to her door."

As for discipline, the children were kept extremely busy and had very little extra time on their hands. When the children did misbehave, Grover would threaten them with his razor strap. A razor strap is a long thick leather strap, possibly two and a half feet in length, used to sharpen a straight razor. Ruby noted that Grover never carried out his threats. Sarah on the other hand, had a switch, which she kept in the kitchen, and she would not hesitate to use it on a misbehaving child.

All of the Etherton children attended a one-room school in the Makanda area named Phelps School from first through eighth grade. Grover had attended this same country school when he was a child. Even Sarah briefly attended Phelps when she first arrived in the area. The student body of Phelps usually numbered from fifteen to twenty students of varying ages and grades. In order to go beyond eighth grade, students had to leave the immediate area. Few of Phelps' graduates traveled to further their education.

This one room school was approximately three-quarters of a mile to a mile from the farm. The Etherton children would walk most days, having to cross two creeks. The water level was such that they could step from one protruding rock to another and make their way across. Occasionally, heavy rain would raise the level of the creeks to a point where the children could not safely cross. On such days, Grover would typically accompany the children along with one of the two mules. The selected mule, Old Jack or Pearl, under Grover's supervision, would transport usually two children at a time on its back across each creek. Saddles were not used. Ruby said, "It was hard to stay on." The child in the front would hang onto the mule's mane. The second child would hang on to the first child. When Old Jack or Pearl was finished with the job, he or she was released and would walk back home.

Automobiles started to appear commonly in the United States in the late teens and early twenties of the twentieth century. Ruby does not remember the first time she saw a car. Up until the time she left the farm, horse and buggy or wagon, or in the case of the Ethertons, mule and wagon, was the prevalent means of transportation in the area. When they would see a car, they would excitedly run after it to get a better look.

Grover had an old truck for just a little while in this time period.

Earl described the truck. "The first family car was a Model-T Ford without a body on it. My father built a box seat in front and a bed on the back for the kids to ride in." The car was never licensed. Grover avoided driving it into town and to other public areas for fear of getting caught.

Ruby remembers her Uncle Hugh Miller regularly drove a car. He was one of the first individuals in the area to make the switch to a "horseless carriage."

One time the family traveled to Carterville in a borrowed two-seater auto that had a cloth roof that folded down and running boards. There were so many Ethertons, that Ruby had to stand on the running board for the duration of the trip, a distance of approximately twenty one miles.

Radio was becoming increasingly popular at this time. The first commercial public broadcasts began in 1920 according to Richard J. Brady in an article on the history of old time radio posted on mysteryshows.com. Mr. Brady also noted that: "Up until the late 1920s, musical programs were most popular with shows highlighting opera, big bands, jazz, classical, and popular music."

Since there was no electricity on the farm, the Ethertons did not have the luxury of a radio. Ruby recalls a trip the family made to her Uncle Will Watson's house specifically to listen to the radio. Will Watson was Grover's half sister's husband. Ruby said it was a special trip. They were all excited and enjoyed listening to the country music broadcast through this unfamiliar electric box.

In the summer after Ruby graduated from the 8th grade, 1928, Grover and Sarah moved to Michigan to work in a factory in order to make additional money. Both worked on the line in a Detroit factory. Ruby could not recall the name of the factory. She did remember that her parents lived in an apartment near what was called Briggs Stadium at the time, later renamed Tiger Stadium. Ruby did remember that their address was 2910 Trumbul. The apartment has since been torn down, as has Tiger Stadium.

That summer of 1929, Ruby was left in charge of the farm. Wayne and Opal had both moved out, making Ruby the oldest in the house at age 14. Ruby's younger siblings, Mary, Earl, and Florence also remained on the farm that summer. Ruby did all of the cooking and was responsible for the management of the house, including supervision of her younger brother and sisters. Ruby said she had her hands full.

A man who lived on a nearby farm was hired to work the farm. Grover and Sarah returned in August so Ruby could go to high school. Incidentally, the great stock market crash of 1929 occurred the following October.

Ruby left the farm at age 14, after she completed 8th grade, to attend high school in Herrin, Illinois. Wayne had previously moved to Carbondale, where he worked for a woman who had some apartments. The woman, in turn, provided him with room and board and helped finance his high school and college education at Southern Illinois University. The high school Wayne attended was on the grounds of SIU. Opal had also moved to Carbondale and lived with Sarah's sister Mina. Opal worked at area restaurants.

2 *High School and College*
Age 14 to Age 21

Older brother Wayne decided Herrin, Illinois would be a good place for Ruby to go to high school. Herrin was approximately 8 miles from the farm. So at age 14, Ruby moved to Herrin where she attended and completed high school. The year of the move was 1929, the year of the great stock market crash and the beginning of the great depression. Ruby noted: "People did not have much money. You were lucky if you had a dime."

Upon arriving in Herrin, Ruby stayed with her mother's sister Lilly Baggett. She stayed with her aunt just a few days until a neighbor offered Ruby a place to lodge if she would help care for the woman's children. The woman had recently separated from her husband and had two young female children to raise, one was a baby. The fourteen-year old Ruby accepted. She had to provide her own food. Ruby's mother would give her two dollars at a time to cover the cost of food for an extended period. At this time, households did not have refrigerators. Some houses in cities did have iceboxes. Iceboxes were so named since they were large wooden insulated boxes cooled with large blocks of ice. Ruby did not have access to an icebox in small town Herrin. She purchased food daily; she had no way of preserving food. Ruby recalls that a meal would cost about ten cents. She often purchased some form of lunchmeat. Occasionally, her Aunt Lilly would provide Ruby with some food, typically soup. The ninth grade Ruby stayed with the neighbor and her girls for about half of a year.

In the middle of Ruby's freshmen year, a lawyer offered her room and board if she would help around his house. Ruby accepted and moved in with the lawyer's family. There were two young male children and caring for them was Ruby's main charge. She also did some house cleaning.

The lawyer had several friends who eagerly employed Ruby as a baby sitter. She earned twenty-five cents per session. Baby-sitting became a major source of income at this time in her life. Ruby continued to baby-sit throughout high school.

Upon returning to high school for her tenth grade year, Ruby began working for a handicapped woman. The woman was confined to a hospital bed. She was able to do very little for herself, could not even feed herself. The husband worked at local coalmines. When Ruby and the husband were both away from the house, a neighbor would periodically check on the confined woman. Ruby stayed with this family for about a year.

In the last two years of high school, Ruby earned room and board working for a coal miner who had three children and a wife who liked to entertain. While Ruby was living with this family, the wife gave birth to a fourth child.

While in high school, Ruby enrolled in a typing class. She had to withdraw. Her fingers consistently swelled to the point of making typing impossible. To this day, she regrets never learning to type.

Ruby's favorite subject in school was art. She later earned a Bachelor of Science Degree with a major in fine arts. She became very adept at drawing and painting pictures featuring natural scenes with pastels, watercolors, or oils.

Ruby did not recall any special after-school events and did not develop any significant high school friendships. She said she worked every minute that she was not in school.

Ruby says her grades were not very good in high school, work got in the way. The responsibilities she assumed in order to earn room and board prevented her from spending the time needed to achieve up to her potential. She did graduate on schedule in 1933 from high school in Herrin.

After graduating, Ruby moved to Fairfield, Illinois to work in a factory that made clothes for Civilian Conservation Corps (CCC) workers. CCC was one of President Franklin Roosevelt's "alphabet agencies," programs initiated to get the country back on its feet from the devastation of the great depression. The specific goal of the CCC was to provide young unemployed men with useful jobs in rural areas related to the conservation and development of natural resources. The young workers planted trees, built earthen dams, repaired and cleaned local, state, and national monuments and parks. The CCC was one of the more popular programs of President Roosevelt's "New Deal."

Fairfield is approximately fifteen miles from Makanda. Ruby's task at the factory was to sew on shirt pockets using an electric sewing machine. It was the first time she ever saw an electric sewing machine. Workers would step on a lever that activated the electricity. Previous sewing machines that Ruby had used required the user to pump a treadle with the right foot to generate power.

Employees of this Fairfield factory were paid on a "piece work" basis. That is, they were paid based on how many items they produced. Ruby said they did not get paid very much. They made less than 3 dollars a day even on good days.

While working at the factory, Ruby stayed for a short time in housing provided for the workers. She and four or five other workers soon moved into a house off site. It was crowded. Ruby slept on the floor. Each boarder paid the owner of the house $2.50 per week for food and lodging.

The factory went out of business soon after Ruby began working for it. She worked at this sewing job for approximately one and a half to two months. She remained in the area through the summer of 1933, securing another child-care job with a local family. Ruby was provided room and board but no pay.

Brother Wayne talked Ruby into moving to Carbondale to attend Southern Illinois University. She began at SIU in the fall of 1933 and received a teaching certificate two to two and a half years later. As she did in high school, Ruby worked for area families caring for children and doing housekeeping for room and board. She continued to make money baby-sitting on the side. Ruby does not think she was well prepared for college and work did continue to get in the way. But, she persisted.

Ruby's "breaking out" continued through college but to a lesser degree. The condition seemed to improve upon leaving the farm, but it did continue. In college, other students were afraid to get near Ruby when she broke-out in hives for fear of catching what she had. A health education professor, Dr. Caldwell, had Ruby sit in the front row of her class and assured the other students that Ruby was not contagious. The professor informed Ruby and her classmates that she apparently had allergies. It was the first time she had ever heard the word allergy.

Physical education credits were required in Ruby's program at SIU. She recalls that she avoided many physical education classes because of her "breaking out" condition. Ruby discovered woman's softball. For this activity, the players remained fully dressed so her hives were not as apparent. Ruby enjoyed playing softball and felt she was quite good at it. She noted that the students at the university called softball "townball." She did not know why. At a point, she was named captain of the team on which she played. There were several teams at the university that her team played against. They did not travel to other universities or colleges. What she described seems similar to present day intramural programs offered at most colleges and universities.

3 *Teaching in One Room Schools, Marriage*
Age 21 to Age 26

After receiving teacher certification, Ruby secured a post at Phelps School, the school she and the other members of the Etherton family had attended from first through eighth grade. Grover and Wayne had also taught briefly at this one room school, one year each. Wayne and Ruby had both received certification from Southern Illinois University, whereas Grover obtained certification by completing a course that lasted only a couple of months. Prior to the teacher certification course, Grover had only completed the eighth grade.

Ruby taught at Phelps for two years, the fall of 1936 through the summer of 1938. The population at Phelps averaged between fifteen to twenty students each year. It was physically impossible for the teacher to get to all the grades each day. Older students helped younger students get through their course materials. Seventh and eighth graders were particularly helpful.

While teaching at Phelps, Ruby stayed at the family farm, since it was approximately three quarters of a mile from the school, except when she stayed at her students' homes. The board of education governing Phelps required their teacher to spend one night each school year with each of his or her students.

There was one family in particular that Ruby regretted staying with each year. The family was not clean. When the dreaded time arrived each year, Sarah would deliver food to Phelps. Ruby would sneak eat and tactfully avoid the food provided by the family. At night, Ruby had to share a bed with the mother of the family, while the father and Ruby's male student slept in the same room in a separate bed.

The next day a tired Ruby and her student returned to their one room school. When the school day was done, Ruby anxiously returned to her home with the fear of possibly transporting bed bugs. Ruby recalled someone bringing bed bugs to their farm one time previously. The Ethertons got rid of the troublesome bugs by ironing all their clothing and bedding. The young teacher recalls thoroughly checking each article of clothes that she had with her. Fortunately, she found no signs of pests either of the two years.

Ruby and other one-room schoolteachers had to do the best with what they had each day. Ruby had students who were older than she was at the time. There were people who would attend school just to have something to do. Ruby recalls having adults come to school to learn to read and write at a basic level. Some adults would attend school to learn how to sign their names.

Ruby recalls a cousin who attended Phelps for a brief period with the intent of learning how to sign his name but gave up. He, in time, declared it was too hard and that he would continue to make an X whenever he needed to sign a paper.

Opal's daughter, Jenny, attended Phelps in first grade while Ruby taught there. Ruby recalls that Jenny did not like the grades that her aunt and teacher had given her on a report sent home, so she simply changed them before giving the report to her parents. Ruby suspects that Wayne encouraged the first grader to do so. Wayne loved to tease and stir things up. A precocious Jenny apparently did not take into account that her aunt might talk with her parents or that there was an official record.

The one room schoolteacher of the day was expected to do a lot more than present academic content. He/she organized and directed the academic and related activities with little direction. It was solely up to the teacher to decide when a student progressed from one grade to the next. There were no standardized tests and few established standards. Letter grades were not used. A very general curriculum guide was provided, but Ruby did not find it very helpful.

Teachers that taught in rural schools in Williamson County were required to attend two meetings chaired by the county superintendent each year: one in the fall and one in the spring. The meetings were held at Marion High School in Marion, Illinois, approximately 21 miles from Phelps School. Ruby rode with fellow area teachers once or twice; one teacher was fortunate enough to have a car. She had to walk a little less than a mile to get to this teacher's house.

Ruby heard from a friend who lived in Carbondale that a man who delivered packages for the United States Postal Service carried passengers. He owned the van he used and charged passengers 25 cents per trip. The route was back and forth from Carbondale to Harrisburg, a distance of about 38 miles each way with stops at Carterville and Marion, two trips a day.

Ruby began using the service to get to the county teacher meetings. There was just one extra seat in the van, and sometimes there were other passengers. Ruby remembers sitting in the back with the packages a number of times. She was usually younger than the other passengers and did not mind sitting in back on one of the boxes.

She would catch a train in nearby Makanda in the evening, get off in Carbondale, spend the night with a friend or relative, and catch a ride in the mail van to Marion the following morning. Then in the afternoon, she would ride in the van on its final return trip to Carbondale, followed by a train trip to Makanda the next day.

The driver and Ruby began dating soon after she started catching occasional rides in the van. The driver's name was James Ownly Owens, although Ruby, as did most people, called him Sy. His mother and father, Artamissia and McClellan Owens, and other members of his family called him Ownly. He hated that name. It was common in the Owens family to refer to the male children by their middle names. James Ownly's or Sy's siblings included Carl, Scott Oland, and Hattie. Born October 6, 1904, James Ownly was the youngest by eight years, 18 years younger than his oldest sibling, Hattie. He was the shortest at 5 feet 11 inches. Carl was probably six feet seven inches tall, Scott, about six feet four inches, and Hattie was approximately six feet tall. The Owens family lived in Harrisburg, Illinois. The source of James Ownly's nickname Sy is unknown. Ruby has no idea when, where, or why people outside the family started calling him Sy. She is not even sure of his nickname's spelling.

Ruby recalls Sy asking his mother about why she gave him the name

Ownly. He said: "Mom why did you name me that? It is not a name, it's only a word." Sy's older brother Carl was originally named Hezekiah. He hated his name too. As a young adult, he legally changed it.

On their first date, Ruby and Sy went to the movies to see a "talkie" in 1937 or 1938. Talkies were movies in which the audience could actually hear the actors talk. The first "talkie" was released in 1927. Previously there were only silent movies, movies with no sound tracks.

The Williamson county superintendent, Don C. Moss, at the bi-annual meetings would tell teachers how to use the required " big green book" to keep records for the year. The "big green book", about the size of an atlas according to Ruby, was used to determine how much money the individual school would receive from the county. In addition to noting enrollment and attendance data, the rural teacher had to make note of any individuals who did not attend school in their catchment area and were of the mandatory school age. Teachers were not allowed to let children younger than six years of age attend school. Students who passed each year would complete the eighth grade at age fourteen, the highest grade offered in this one-room school. To go beyond the eighth grade, students would need to leave the area. Few went beyond the eighth grade. Mr. Moss also instructed teachers as to how to best deal with specific discipline concerns and how to deal with any usual or unusual situations that might arise in their schools.

Seven years or so later, during World War II, Ruby needed to get confirmation from Williamson County that she had taught in the county in order to secure employment in the engineering department at the bomber plant in Ypsilanti, Michigan. The young female clerk who Ruby approached could find no records to verify Ruby's county teaching experience. Ruby asked about the old "big green books" that they were required to keep up to date and were collected at the end of each school year. The young woman checked and found Ruby's record books. This served as the proof she was seeking.

In addition to organizing and directing the activities of the day, the teacher had to see to it that the school was kept clean and that the fire kept going when the temperature dictated. The process of setting up wood or coal in preparation for a fire was called "laying the fire." Ruby would "lay the fire" after school for the next day. The school was rarely locked.

Ruby remembers that fox hurters would occasionally use the school on weekends. They stayed in the school seeking warmth while their dogs hunted and chased fox. The appreciative hunters, typically, after using the prepared logs or coal, would return the favor and also "lay a fire."

As was the case in most one room rural schools, there was a bell tower over the entrance to Phelps that contained a very large bell. Ruby rang the bell at the start and end of the school day, 9 a.m. and 4 p.m., by pulling the long thick rope attached to the bell. Local farmers would set their wind-up clocks upon hearing the school bell. There was no electricity at the time in the area, and the clocks were not very reliable.

A hand held bell was used to sound the end of recess and lunch. There was a ten to fifteen minute recess each morning and each afternoon. Lunch period lasted one hour. Baseball was one of the favored free time activities.

As for water, the students and teacher at Phelps depended on a cistern, which was supplied from the run off of rainwater from the school's roof. There was no other source of water. The cistern was a six to ten foot hole lined with rocks. The opening was covered with a wooden frame. No pulley; just an eight to ten foot piece of rope attached to a bucket.

The process of bringing the water from the cistern to the surface was called to "draw water." Ruby would "draw water" several times a day, usually to provide drinking water. Occasionally students would bring tin cups to school for drinking, but usually they all drank from the same dipper. Since the water came from a cistern, it tasted better right after it rained, according to Ruby.

One time Ruby noticed a third grader whom she described as her second cousin, Ivan Watson, looking up in the bell tower. When asked what he was looking at, Ivan responded, "I see a fire up there." Ruby looked and indeed saw fire. She quickly summoned the older male students, put the ladder in the bell tower, and developed a line to pass the water with the solitary bucket back and forth from the cistern to the small fire. In short order, Ruby's bucket brigade had put out the fire and had averted a major disaster. There was only one door at Phelps and that was directly below the bell tower. Ruby suspects the wood fire from the school's stove was somehow the source of the fire, but the source was never really investigated or determined.

Phelps was located in the middle of a field. The nearest road was a quarter to half of a mile away. Ruby recalls that when the county superintendent would visit the school, he would park on the side of a road then would have to walk through fields to get to Phelps. She only remembers him making the trip once in her two years at the school.

The Works Progress Administration (WPA) was a public program intended to provide employment for some of those in need during the great depression. One of their projects was to construct outdoor toilets for the rural schools. In Ruby's second year at Phelps, a "WPA toilet" was constructed. A large hole was dug and lined with concrete then covered with a new wooden structure. This was considered a vast improvement over the old shabby "outhouse" they had previously. Sears and Montgomery Ward catalogs served as toilet paper.

One time while teaching at Phelps, Ruby served as an arbiter in a dispute over the price of lumber. The disagreement involved the young teacher's Uncle Hugh Miller and a local farmer, Holly Craig, who could neither read nor write. The two decided to let the local teacher decide on the correct price. They approached Ruby in the middle of the school day. She told them she could not possibly do the necessary calculations while caring for the students. The two men directed the children outside to allow Ruby time to figure out the price. Once the calculations were complete, the men readily accepted the price and went on their way.

Grover, who had a portable lumber mill, had taught his children how to figure out the prevailing price of lumbered wood. When Ruby returned to the farm after school and told her family the story, her brother Wayne became extremely upset. He did not think Ruby could possibly do the calculations correctly. The disturbed Wayne could not sleep or eat. He demanded to review the calculations. When he did so, to his surprise and Ruby's delight, Wayne agreed with the price she had determined.

Near Christmas recess, the students at Phelps had a tradition of locking the teacher out of the school until the teacher provided treats. The treats typically consisted of candy, oranges, and maybe apples. The trick was to beat the teacher to school on the assigned day. Ruby is proud that they never arrived before she did. They were never able to lock her out. She did, however, provide the expected treats to the disappointed students each year.

In 1938, the state of Illinois started buying area farms for the Crab Orchard Recreational Area Project. It was thought that Phelps would be closed. Ruby secured her second one room teaching position in a country school near Chester, a small town approximately fifty miles from Makanda. In contrast to Phelps, this school was accessible by road and had a hand pump to draw underground water. This school also had a WPA toilet. In fact, Phelps functioned for one more year with just five or fewer students. The Etherton's Williamson County farm was purchased in 1939 by the state.

Currently Crab Orchard is listed as both a state park and a national refuge. Its website noted that it contains 44,000 acres of land and water, and that the present annual visitation rate is approximately one million people.

Wayne located an available farm approximately 25 miles south of Makanda in Union County. Wayne was teaching at a one-room school in the vicinity at the time. Grover and Sarah purchased and moved to the Union County farm in 1939. It has remained in the Etherton family to date. Wayne's son and daughter-in-law, Bill and Judy Etherton, currently live on this farm.

Ruby spent just one difficult year at the one room school near Chester. A particularly large and mean older student, Leo, was consistently problematic. He was a lot bigger than the five foot one inch Ruby. One time Leo decided to give his young teacher a whipping. As he approached to administer said whipping, a concerned Ruby was stirring the coal in the school's furnace. Ruby resolutely raised the iron poker, looked Leo in the eye and said, "I'll let you have it." Leo backed off.

This county's superintendent, a man with the last name of Etherton, had suggested Ruby suspend Leo. He had given her instructions as to how to do so. Incidentally, Ruby did not know if or how she and the superintendent were related. After the poker incident, Ruby did not feel a need to carry out the suspension, although Leo remained somewhat difficult. Leo's mother's infant child had accidently been killed, and the mother felt responsible. Ruby did not want to contribute to her misery.

The evening after the confrontation, Ruby relayed the details of the incident to a school board member with whom she boarded while at the school near Chester. She found him to be very supportive. Nonetheless,

Ruby departed from this one room school after receiving an offer from another rural one room school, Fly School. The school board of Fly School offered her considerably more money, a little shy of one hundred dollars per month, 1939 dollars, for eight months. Ruby accepted the offer and remained at this Makanda area school for two years, from the fall of 1939 to spring of 1941. Fly was located about one quarter of a mile from the recently built Giant City State Park Lodge.

One Room School Students and Ruby
Taken in 1941 at Fly School
Ruby is top center

According to the Illinois Department of Natural Resources website, the State of Illinois in 1927 acquired 1,100 acres of land in neighboring Union and Jackson counties on which a park was developed and the lodge was built. The construction of the rustic lodge and twelve cabins was completed in 1936; a Civilian Conservation Corps project. The park later expanded to 4,000 acres.

Ruby recalls that the school year for rural schools was notably shorter than it is today, seven to eight months. For that matter, what Ruby refers to as "town schools" of the day had a lengthier school year. The schools at which she taught started in early September and ended in April. The students came from farms and were expected to work on them. School was rarely a priority. Ruby earned less than $100 per month each year she taught in one-room schools. She believes she was one of the better-paid rural teachers, since her family knew people on each of the school boards. Teachers, at the time, would have to independently negotiate or accept the offer of the local school board. In the summer months, Ruby returned to Southern Illinois University to continue her work towards a Bachelor of Science Degree.

Ruby age 24 before they married   *Sy age 35 before they married*

Ruby and Sy were married on February 17, 1940. Ruby was teaching at Fly School at the time. Sy continued driving the mail transport van. He was thirty-five years of age and Ruby was twenty-four. The couple crossed the border to be married in Charleston, Missouri. They kept their marriage a secret for a time. By marrying in Missouri, the announcement of the wedding was not reported in the local Illinois newspapers. Sy was afraid that if their friends learned of their marriage, they would do a chivaree at the couple's residence. In a chivaree, or "belling," friends and neighbors of a newly married couple would make a lot of noise banging on pots and pans, ringing bells, and blowing horns with the intent of rousing the newlyweds. The expectation was that the noisemakers would eventually be invited in for refreshments. Sy and Ruby did manage to avoid the dreaded chivaree.

4 Living in Chicago, The Bomber Plant, First Child
Age 26 to Age 31

The couple's marriage remained a secret up to the time they left Southern Illinois, moving to Chicago a few months after their marriage. Carl Owens secured a job for his younger brother in the state's largest city. Ruby does not recall the specifics of this job. Sy made the move in the spring, whereas Ruby completed the year at Fly school then joined her husband in the early summer of 1940.

Soon after moving to Chicago, Ruby began working at a sewing factory. She remembers that they were in desperate need for workers. Since Ruby had experience, they hired her immediately. Ruby had used an electric sewing machine to sew pockets on shirts soon after graduating from high school. This factory, which made clothes for the military, was located in southern Chicago. Ruby said she was "pretty good" at sewing with an electric machine. She noted the tasks were very repetitive, and she was rather fast.

Ruby vividly recalls one particular day in which the owner of the factory ordered the workers to turn off all the machines. He then turned on a radio, and they listened as the president of the United States, Franklin Roosevelt, declared war on Japan. This was December 8, 1941, the day after the Japanese attacked Pearl Harbor. The workers, including Ruby, were not surprised that the country was going to war. This news was expected sooner, rather than later.

Sy's job was on the north side of Chicago. He would ride the "EL", the city's elevated rail system, to and from work each day. The couple initially stayed with Sy's brother but soon found an apartment on the south side of Chicago on 62nd Street near Drexel. They lived just a few doors down from the Trianon Ballroom. The Trianon was said to be Chicago's most expensive and most extravagant hall when it opened in 1922.

Ruby recalls seeing the big jazz bands unloading their equipment behind the famous ballroom. The couple enjoyed sitting on their front porch, as did many of their neighbors, listening to the era's popular big band music. The bands played at night and practiced during the day. The people in the neighborhood could hear the bands nearly as well as the paid ticket holders, Ruby believes.

The University of Chicago was near the couple's apartment. Ruby said the grounds of the university were very nice, park like. She has pleasant memories of her, Sy, and others having picnics on the university's well cared for green lawns under the shade of beautiful big trees.

In their second year in Chicago, Sy became very ill. He suffered from what was called a "nervous breakdown." He was admitted and remained in a hospital in a nearby suburb for about two months. Ruby's older sister Opal suggested that they move to Michigan and stay with her and her husband, Mike Losacco, in their house near the Willow Run Bomber Plant, east of Ypsilanti. Opal said she would take care of Sy when Ruby was away at work. Ruby accepted her sister's generous offer. She and Sy moved to Michigan in 1943.

The war effort was in full swing. The Willow Run Bomber Plant, being one of the country's largest plants, was a very busy place. Mike Losacco worked at the plant, as did Ruby's younger sister Mary and her husband, Jim Fox. Mike, Jim, and Mary worked with nearly 43,000 people assembling B-24 bombers, or Liberators, as they were called. At peak production, a plane an hour came off the line. President and Mrs. Roosevelt traveled to Willow Run to praise the workers for their contribution to the war effort.

Soon after moving to Michigan, Ruby joined her relatives at the plant. She, because of her college education and art background, was assigned to the engineering department. Her specific task was to draw up specifications for the nose of the B-24H bomber, a modified B-24. Engineers would tell her what they wanted and her task was to draw the specifics onto the plans or blueprints. She was called a detailer. Ruby felt considerable stress in this job. She feared that if she made a mistake, it would be too costly. Human life was at stake. After six weeks or so in the engineering department, Ruby requested and was granted a transfer to the assembly line.

Sy's health was much improved within a month of the couple's move to Michigan. Thus, he decided to join the others on the line at the bomber plant. In order to get a job at the plant, Sy had to have a birth certificate. There was no official record of his birth. Sy was born in a rural area a few miles outside of Harrisburg, Illinois. On one of several trips back to his hometown, Sy sought a birth certificate. He and his mother, Artamissia Owens, traveled to the county offices to obtain the needed certificate. The official in charge would not just take their word for the specifics of the birth. They needed some proof. So, Sy and his mother took the official out into the country to see an "old woman" that still lived near Sy's birthplace and had witnessed the birth.

The official, after talking with the "old woman," made out the birth certificate. Confusion about Sy's official name started at this point. Previously, it was thought his name was James Ownly Owens. The official, on the certificate, wrote Ownly James Owens. The name that Sy detested became his official first name. Subsequently, he signed checks, O. James Owens.

Ruby and Sy stayed with Opal, Michael Losacco, and their two children, Jenny Louise and Michael Grover for a little less than a year. They shared the Losacco's house, which was located on Ecorse Road in Belleville, Michigan. Mary and Jim Fox stayed in a trailer they owned, which they kept on the Losacco property. Ruby said it was crowded at times.

Jenny Losacco was born March 13, 1931, making her the oldest of her generation on the Etherton side of the family. Michael Losacco, or Mikie, as he is usually called, was born August 18, 1938. Ruby noted that she gave Mikie his first bath.

While staying with the Losaccos, Ruby remembers that five-year old Mikie got lost one time. All those that were home frantically looked for the lost boy. They feared that he might have crossed Ecorse Road on which there was often a good deal of traffic. In time, to the family's collective relief, they found Mikie hidden in a closet fast asleep.

When asked if he remembered the closet incident, Mikie noted that he did and provided additional information. He said he recalled taking a big piece of cheese and a blanket into the closet and locking the door, leaving the skeleton key facing inward. He remained hidden for quite awhile. He ate the cheese then took a nap.

Ruby's brothers, Wayne and Earl, both joined the military at the beginning of World War II. Earl's youngest son, Bob Etherton, was the source of the military history for both his uncle and father.

Bob believes Wayne entered the army as a Second Lieutenant, was promoted to First Lieutenant, and eventually became a Captain. Bob suspects Wayne might have been awarded his captain's bars while serving in the reserves after the war, but he is not sure. Wayne served in the European theater in a combat engineering group. As such, Wayne's company would have tasks such as installing temporary bridges, reinforcing damaged structures, construction of fortifications, and/or demolishing enemy structures. At one point, Wayne was injured by an explosive device and spent a week or so in a field hospital.

Bob Etherton believes his father, Earl, chose to join the navy rather than be drafted into the army. Ruby's younger brother began his military service at the navy's boot camp and large training facility in Chicago, named Great Lakes. Earl's rating, or job specialty, was Aviation Metal Smith. Earl, in this capacity, learned to make repairs on aircraft structures and skins, working with aluminum (the primary material), rivets, welding, brazing, and sheet metal. Bob noted that his father found this work "both interesting and satisfying." Earl was soon made an instructor at the Great Lakes facility.

In time, Earl wanted to move on, "not wanting to remain stuck as an instructor for the whole war." Accordingly, he requested and was granted a transfer to Naval Air Station in Sanford, Florida. At the time of his transfer, Earl was a Petty Officer, 3rd Class. At Sanford, Earl applied his training and related experience from the farm, working on real airplanes. Earl was apparently quite adept as an Aviation Metal Smith. Soon after transferring to this Florida base, he was assigned to the most difficult repairs there. Upon his discharge from the navy, Earl had obtained the rank of Aviation Metal Smith, First Class.

Sarah and Grover remained on the farm in Union County during the war. Florence had also moved to Michigan. Ruby remembers going to Florence's wedding while she was living in Chicago. Her youngest sister married a Michigan native, Art Casmer. The couple resided in the Dearborn area. Art worked for Ford Motor Company at its River Rouge plant. Ruby recalls that Florence was pregnant at the time she and Sy lived with Opal. Florence gave birth to her only child, Ronald William Casmer, commonly called Ronnie, March 1, 1943.

Ronnie's mother, and/or possibly one of his aunts, told him of a time when Ruby changed his diaper. Ronnie noted, "I (apparently) engaged in a bit of 'target-practice' and hit Aunt Ruby square in the mouth with a strong yeller stream. To this day, I am not entirely sure if I have been forgiven."

Ruby figures Sarah and Grover did very little farming after their children left the farm. Grover's health was in decline. Ruby attributes the decline to excessive tobacco use and an unhealthy diet. Ruby remembers Grover frequently falling asleep, then waking after choking on the ever present wad of tobacco in his mouth. He did not particularly enjoy eating vegetables. He really liked and consumed a lot of fried potatoes. Much of what he ate was fried. Grover would say; he wanted food that would stick to his ribs.

Grover's 67ᵗʰ birthday and 47ᵗʰ anniversary celebration
Seated: Parents—Grover and Sarah
Standing: Etherton Children left to right—Earl, Ruby, Wayne, Florence, Opal

Grover's 67ᵗʰ birthday and 47ᵗʰ anniversary celebration
Grover in front, Sarah standing behind

After Sy started working at Willow Run, Ruby began looking for an apartment. The influx of workers to the area flooded the housing and apartment markets. In general, finding housing was one of the most serious problems for the workers at the bomber plant. Some had to resort to sharing their living spaces in an off-shift arrangement called "hot beds", meaning they only had accommodations when they were not working.

In time, the persistent Ruby found an apartment in the upstairs of a house on the east side of Dearborn, Michigan, just off Michigan Avenue. So, the couple moved to their own three-room apartment. Ruby believes the rent payment might have been twenty-five dollars a month. Sy continued working at Willow Run, commuting from Dearborn to work each day for a short time, a distance of about sixteen miles. Ruby quit her job directly after the move.

Ruby gave birth to their first child, Judy Ellen Owens, while in

38

Dearborn. Judy was born September 28, 1944 in a small hospital in West Dearborn called Dearborn Medical Center, very near the Detroit border. Their landlord had recommended a doctor named Charles Castrop, who was affiliated with this hospital.

Judy was given her maternal grandmother's middle name. Many people called Sarah Etherton, Ella, a nickname from Ellen.

Sy, in particular, really enjoyed listening to a singer/comedienne named Judy Canova, a popular figure on the radio at the time. Judy Canova was nicknamed the Queen of the Air in 1949. The radio star's birth name was Juliette Canova. In a mini biography posted on the imdb.com website, it was noted: "Her outlandish country bumpkin image may be considered tacky and/or offensive by today's measure, but back in the 1930s and 1940s it worked." Accordingly, Ruby and Sy named their first child Judy, not Judith or Juliette for that matter.

Ruby recalls making diapers for Judy. It was difficult to find diapers during World War II as material was in short supply. There was a yard goods store in Dearborn near the family's apartment. The owners of the store would save flannelette, a white flannel material that was fuzzy on one side. Due to wartime shortages, they would only sell her two yards at a time from which Ruby would make three diapers.

Both of Ruby's brothers became fathers in 1944, as well. Wayne's wife Lillian gave birth to William Wayne Etherton, Jr., most frequently called Bill, January 14th. Earl's wife Maxine, nicknamed Mickey, delivered Jimmie Nelson Etherton, usually referred to as Jim, November 1st. Lillian and Wayne's second child, Sue Ann Etherton, was born on September 7, 1946.

Ruby recalls that Lillian and baby Bill stayed on the farm with Sarah and Grover when Wayne first went overseas. Ruby remembers being told of a time that Lillian was hanging clothes up to dry and Bill was lying on the ground near the clothes line. Bill could not walk yet. A rooster charged him. Lillian grabbed a club and hit the aggressive bird before it reached the baby. The rooster lay unconscious. An upset Lillian with baby in hand approached her mother-in-law with tears in her eyes and said, "I believe I killed your rooster." Sarah laughed and said "We'll have chicken and dumplings for dinner."

The fighting ended in World War II when the Japanese surrendered,

August 14th, 1945. It was preceded by the dropping of two atomic bombs on Japan by the United States. Ceremonial surrender occurred September 2nd. When asked for her reaction to the dropping of the bomb at the time Ruby responded, "I don't remember."

By some accounts, the workers at Willow Run were so productive that the plant needed to shed workers sooner than expected, well before the war was over. The author's mother-in-law, Patricia Smith Balkam, kept detailed records of events in her life. She also worked at the bomber plant in this time period. Her starting pay was $.85 per hour. She worked in an office. When she left Willow Run her pay had increased to $1.15 per hour, a very good wage for the time. Based on Patte's records, lay-offs began on July 13, 1944. The employees were so angered that a walkout occurred two days later.

Sy was laid-off. Soon after the lay-off, a friend of Sy's, who had a job with Detroit Edison, suggested Sy apply for a job with the large Detroit-based utility. He did so and was hired. He was trained to make a special type of concrete and became quite adept. Edison sent him to construction sites from Monroe to Port Huron in southeastern Michigan, one side of Michigan to the other. Sy was offered supervising positions through the years but repeatedly refused such offers.

The Owens family stayed in the Dearborn apartment for about two and a half years. The owners of the house had initially decided to rent the upstairs for the income. In time they felt cramped, as their four boys grew bigger. They decided they needed the upstairs back.

Ruby and Sy found a small house in Romulus, Michigan on Essex Street. Ruby believes they paid about $2500 for the house, possibly in 1947. They were only there for a short time, a year to a year and a half, before a young newly married couple asked to buy the small house. The house only had one decent size bedroom.

Judy's crib barely fit in a second room that was a little bigger than a closet, according to Ruby. There was no way that a full size bed would fit in the room. When the young couple expressed an interested in the house, Ruby and Sy saw an opportunity and sold the house and property. The house was just too small.

While in search of a new home, Ruby, Sy, and young Judy moved in with Ruby's youngest sister Florence's family in nearby Taylor,

Michigan. In a short time, Ruby and Sy found a small house in Romulus, Michigan, 8258 Farnum, in time for Judy to start school. The house was located within a half of a mile of a small airport, named Wayne County Airport, which was undergoing a major expansion. The significantly enlarged airport, in time, became Michigan's main airport and a major international airport. The airport was renamed Detroit Metropolitan Wayne County Airport in 1958 according to the airport's website. The Owens family made the move and remained in this Romulus home until 1966, about 17 years.

5 *Living in Romulus, 2ⁿᵈ Child, Father's Death*
Age 31 to Age 37

When Ruby, Sy, and Judy moved into the small house on Farnum Street in Romulus, there was no running water. Fortunately, the family found the next-door neighbors, the Nichols, to be very friendly and helpful. The Nichols invited their new neighbors to get water from their outdoor spigot or from a utility room sink whenever they wanted to do so. The Owens family depended on the Nichols for water from the fall of 1948 through the following spring. By the spring, Ruby was substitute teaching, providing additional income; making possibly $10 per day. Thus, they contracted to have a water line installed connecting their home to the township's water supply.

Prior to connecting to township water, the Owens family used a water bucket to carry water from the Nichols' to their new home. As for bathing, they took what Ruby called "sponge baths." Actually, they did not use a sponge. Instead, Ruby said they used "wash rags" and soap. They had no tub, just a small metal pan. They would heat the wash water by putting the water-filled pan on top of a small heating stove located in the kitchen. In the kitchen, a bucket of water was kept specifically for drinking. A dipper with a long metal handle was placed near the bucket. They either drank directly from the dipper or would transfer the water into glasses.

Ruby noted that both she and Sy were accustomed to living without running water in the house. On the Etherton farm, there was never any running water while Ruby lived there. Sy lived in a small city but did not have running water. Ruby pointed out that Sy's family home was hooked up to city water, but the pipe was broken all the time she was around. Ruby is not sure when the pipe initially broke. When they visited Dad's sister, who as an adult had moved back into the family home, in the nineteen fifties and sixties, she still did not have running water even then. There was a manual hand pump in the kitchen. An outhouse was located behind the house. Ruby recalls Artamissia Owens, her mother-in-law, never wanted the weeds cut behind the house, and they grew to be very tall at times. She did not want people seeing her go to the outhouse.

The Farnum Street house consisted of a living room, a kitchen, and two bedrooms. There was an oil burning stove in the living room and a small stove in the kitchen, which burned either wood or coal. They had what Ruby described as a chemical toilet, no outhouse. Each evening, when the ground was not frozen, they would dig a hole in the backyard in which the contents of the "chemical toilet" were dumped. When the ground was too hard to dig in, they discretely dumped the contents in the adjoining unoccupied field.

A few years after moving into the Romulus house, a first cousin of Ruby's built an addition consisting of a small bedroom, an indoor toilet, a furnace room, and a utility room. They also installed a septic tank in the back yard. The cousin, Noel Gibson, had moved from Southern Illinois to the area in search of employment.

Sy's mother died in 1949. His father, McClellan, had died eleven years previously at age 74. Prior to Artamissia's death, the Owens family would return to Southern Illinois at least once a month, a distance of 550 to 600 miles. Ruby noted that Sy's mother, "Ma," thought they should visit more often. Artamissia, Ruby said, was unaware of the distance from Michigan to Southern Illinois.

Mikie Losacco recalls traveling with Ruby and Sy on one of their weekend trips to Southern Illinois as a child. Sy did all the driving. Ruby did not have a license at the time. Mikie vividly remembers that Sy drove so slowly, and he would stop for coffee and a piece of pie often. Mikie thought they would never get there. Ruby confirmed, Sy might stop three or four times for coffee and often times order a piece of pie on their trips. Ruby does not recall how long it took to get to Southern Illinois from Michigan. There were no expressways at the time, and the route was not as direct as it is today. Currently, the trip takes about ten hours, including brief stops for food and fuel.

Judy recalls visiting Artamissia in her Granger Street home in

Harrisburg, Illinois as a four year old. Judy remembers sitting on her grandmother's bed and talking with her one day, waking up the next day and discovering that the bed and her grandmother were gone. Judy said her grandmother "seemed just fine" when the two had talked.

The eighty-three year old Artamissia had died in the middle of the night. Ruby suspects the bed had been moved to an out-building the family called the icehouse. Sy's brother Scott was also at home at the time of their mother's death. Ruby recalls that she, Sy, and Judy had slept in the dining room that night.

Ruby noted that Sy wanted to get the funeral over quickly. He had difficulty dealing with funerals in general, let alone one for his mother. Artamissia's body was laid out in the Granger Street house's living room for visitation one day and taken to a church for a service the following morning.

Sy and Ruby had moved into the house on Farnum Street in time for Judy to start kindergarten in Romulus. From the forms that were filled out, the officials in the Romulus District Schools learned that Ruby had an Illinois teaching certificate. Ruby said they were desperate for teachers at the time. They really wanted her to teach full time. Judy was in school for just half of a day. Ruby agreed to do a limited amount of substitute teaching. They needed the money.

On July 2, 1949, Ruby gave birth to her second child, James McClelland Owens. It was a very hot summer. Ruby returned to Dr. Castrop and the Dearborn Medical Center for the delivery. The United States was in the early stages of the baby boom period following World War II. The hospital was crowded. Four women were crammed into rooms intended for two. When running out of baby beds, hospital personnel put newborns in cabinet drawers.

Ruby is not sure, but she believes Sy, after taking her to the hospital, took four year old Judy to a Detroit Tiger baseball game. He certainly did not stay around for the delivery. It was not expected for a husband to view the delivery at the time.

I was named after my father and my paternal grandfather. Ruby says Sy's family had a tendency to put the "d" sound on words, even if they did not end with a d. Thus, she assumed McClellan ended with a d as she spelled out my name for the birth certificate.

Romulus school officials continued to eagerly pursue Ruby for a full time teaching position. Ruby was nonetheless reluctant to sign a contract. The principal of one of the elementary schools had once told the superintendent, Mr. Eiker, in Ruby's presence, that she just liked the way Ruby walked into a class and took charge.

Superintendent Eiker, on several occasions, attempted to sell Ruby on the idea of accepting a full time position. There was a fifth grade class at Romulus Elementary that had a number of difficult male students in it. Some of the boys were bigger than Ruby. She did not enjoy this class. Mr. Eiker told the principal and Ruby that if she didn't sign a contract, he would just place her with this difficult class for the remainder of the year.

Mrs. Nichols, the next-door neighbor, had no children. She desperately wanted to have children. She encouraged Ruby to accept the school district's offer. She would happily take care of me while Ruby was at school. I was still nursing and had to learn how to use a bottle. So in the middle of the 1950-51 school year, Ruby started what ended up being a long career with the Romulus School District, teaching at the elementary level.

Ruby at this time did not have a driver's license. The school officials told her not to worry. They would see to it that she got to and from school each day. For about a year and a half, a district school bus would pick Ruby up in the morning and take her home after school on a daily basis.

In Ruby's first full time teaching assignment, she was assigned to two elementary schools, Airport and Texas. Both schools have long since been torn down. Each school had a principal who doubled as a third grade teacher, Beatrice Dittmar and Virginia Roberts. Ruby would relieve one principal from classroom responsibilities in the morning, catch a ride on the half-day kindergarten bus then relieve the second principal in the afternoon.

Ruby was assigned to two half-day sessions of kindergarten classes at Airport Elementary the next school year. Judy remembers hearing her second grade teacher tell another teacher that Judy was the daughter of the new teacher at Airport. To Ruby's and the district's surprise, one hundred students showed up for kindergarten on the first day.

The district soon assigned a second kindergarten teacher to Airport to accommodate the large influx of new students.

Many of the new students came from temporary housing set-up near Detroit Wayne County Airport. Most of the adults from this housing area worked at the Willow Run plant. They were migrants from rural southern states, many from Kentucky. They were poor. Some had never seen a bathtub. Some of the children initially slept in the tubs.

Ruby noted that recent migrants to the area needed clothing. She remembers that the little girls would often come to school without panties under their dresses. The kids rarely wore socks.

Ruby donated her children's used clothing to her students. She additionally had a box in which she gathered donations from friends and fellow teachers. She and Sy delivered a donated sleeping mattress to a family one time. Ruby said that Sy would not go into the house because of its condition.

Prior to moving to Michigan, Ruby had completed the equivalent of approximately three years of college credit. She earned two years credit while working on her Illinois teaching certificate and proceeded to take classes during summer vacations while teaching in one-room schools in Southern Illinois. All of her college credits before the move to Michigan came from Southern Illinois University.

While teaching in Romulus, Ruby took night and summer classes at Michigan State Normal College in Ypsilanti, previously named Michigan State Normal School. The Normal School was established in 1849, and the first set of students started attending classes in 1853, one hundred twenty-two individuals. The school underwent three name changes from 1849 to the present, each reflecting the changing status of the school. Michigan State Normal School became Michigan State Normal College in 1899, Eastern Michigan College in 1956, and Eastern Michigan University in 1959.

Ruby received her Bachelor of Science degree July 29, 1955, specializing in fine arts and elementary education from Michigan State Normal College. After graduation, she continued to take evening and summer classes. On August 18, 1967, she received her Master of Arts degree in education from Eastern Michigan University. In later years, Judy and I both also earned bachelor's and master's degrees at EMU.

The tradition continued into the third generation when Judy's daughter, Jennifer Leonard, earned a Bachelor of Science degree in social work at Eastern in 1996.

Sy purchased a second used car about a year and a half after Ruby started teaching in Romulus. Initially, Ruby and Sy made an arrangement with Bea Dittmar, the principal of Airport Elementary, whereby Mrs. Dittmar would use the car to drive her and Ruby to and from school each day. Bea kept the car at her house. Ruby no longer depended on the district for transportation. In a few months, she obtained a driver's license, taking a drivers training course at Romulus High School. Her instructor was Harold Cass. Several years later, just prior to our sixteenth birthdays, Judy and I also had driver's training with Mr. Cass, a memorable character.

Ruby remembers our neighbor, Mrs. Nichols, wanted to have her kitchen wall-papered. Mr. Nichols worked long hours and could not find the time. Mrs. Nichols did not consider doing it herself. Ruby volunteered. After finishing the wallpapering, Ruby and Mrs. Nichols decided the ceiling needed painting. Ruby just got up on her neighbor's kitchen table and started painting. At a point, Mrs. Nichols got up on the table herself, the table collapsed. Ruby noted that Mrs. Nichols was a bit overweight.

Grover's health was in decline. In 1949, he traveled to the Detroit area to visit his children who had migrated there and to have his health reviewed by professionals. He was examined at Henry Ford Hospital in October of that year. In the medical report the hospital prepared, it was noted that Grover was mildly obese, being 5 feet 9 inches tall and weighing $196\frac{3}{4}$ lbs., had high blood pressure and heart problems. His blood pressure was measured at 170 over 110.

The report noted a discussion with Grover about the "necessity of living within your cardiac reserve, avoiding anything that causes you anginal distress." It was also suggested that he decrease salt intake and reduce starch in his diet in order to loose weight. When Ruby was asked if Grover followed the recommendations, she said "nope." When asked if he had changed his life style at all, she said "no way." Grover died four years later.

Grover died on September 21, 1952 at age sixty-seven. Ruby and

I traveled to the family farm in Southern Illinois by bus. I was three years old and have no recollection of the event. Judy and Sy stayed in Romulus. Mrs. Nichols cared for Judy when Sy was away at work.

The Etherton's farm was located on a road between Dongola and Mill Creek, about four miles from Dongola and a little more than a mile and a half from Mill Creek. The family joined the Baptist church in Mill Creek soon after moving to the area in the late 1930s. It was not unusual for Sarah and others to walk to and from the church. Grover rarely attended services. When he died, the visitation and funeral services were held in the Mill Creek Baptist Church. Ruby recalls that it was extremely hot in Mill Creek that day.

When the Ethertons moved to the Union County farm in 1939, Ruby recalls there being a hotel, a post office, two churches, a sawmill and a few stores in Mill Creek. It was on a railroad line and trains regularly stopped in the village. Earl's son, Ruby's nephew, Jim grew up on a farm adjacent to the original Union County farm and still lives in the area. Jim continues to witness a village in decline. When he was a child, he remembers there were two stores, a tiny post office, a sawmill, two churches, and a country school (one room). Presently, he explained there are only a few houses and a relocated Baptist church. The 2000 census found seventy-six residents living in twenty-nine houses. By 2010, the population had declined to sixty-five.

The Allen brothers owned and operated the area sawmill. The two lived in an old house in Mill Creek near their mill. Wayne's son, Bill, and his wife, Judy, currently live on the family farm and had also lived there when they attended Southern Illinois University as undergraduates. One day as they were passing through Mill Creek on the way to SIU, Bill and Judy saw a man's "bare butt" hanging out of a window in the Allen house. Certainly they thought it was strange, especially since it was in the middle of the day. When they returned to the farm in the evening they learned one of the brothers had died and was found in a window of his house.

6 Life on Farnum Street, The Third Child
Age 37 to Age 47

The Owens family was one of the first in their neighborhood in Romulus to buy a television set. It had a very small screen and was encased in a stand-alone big wooden box. Sy really enjoyed watching baseball games and prize fights.

A neighbor, Mr. Price, often viewed the games and fights with Sy. Mr. Price was an enthusiastic fan. Ruby said he frequently jumped out of his seat and yelled at the television. It was quite a sight. He talked to the television set as if the people on the screen could hear him. Mr. Price, as did Sy, smoked cigarettes. Ruby recalls that he was typically so excited that he neglected to use an ashtray; just letting the ashes fall from the cigarette while in his mouth, be it on the floor or the furniture.

Ruby recalls that the Daly Drive-in was the first drive-in restaurant she ever saw. Art Casmer, Ruby's brother-in-law and husband of Florence, was a good friend of the owner, Bill Ihlenfeldt. According to the Daly Restaurant's website, the first restaurant was built on Jim Daly Road, the source of the name, in Dearborn Heights. It was located very near the Casmer home in Taylor, Michigan. Ruby became a friend of the sister of the owner, Doris (Ihlenfeldt) Grace, in later years. At one time, there were eighteen Daly Drive-ins in the Detroit area. Currently, the restaurant located on Plymouth Road in Livonia is the only Daly restaurant in operation.

Drive-in restaurants were extremely popular in the 1950s. The increasingly automobile dependent population of the time created a market for restaurants such as the Daly Drive-in. At Daly's and others like it throughout the country, a patron would simply drive up in a car, order food and drink, and a car-hop would deliver it on a custom made tray which was hung from the car window. The customer never had to leave the car. Drive-in restaurants began to fade from the American landscape with the introduction of fast food in the United States by McDonald's, Burger King and other chains.

Ruby figures her experience in country schools helped prepare her for much of what she faced in the Romulus schools. There was one thing that she had no experience with in the country schools: head lice. In her Romulus classes, at times, they were rampant. Ruby became quite adept at finding lice in the hair of the affected students. She would part a student's hair with two combs exposing the roots and search for the lice nits, clusters of eggs, with toothpicks. Unlike today, the use of rubber gloves was not even considered. Upon finding lice, the school would contact the students' parents and advise them as to how to get rid of the troublesome pests. Ruby recalls a principal once brought her a box of toothpicks and explained that she would need to inspect all the students of the school. They had to do something.

Ruby taught at Airport Elementary for just two years. The soldiers and temporary workers eventually left the Wayne County Airport area. Airport Elementary was closed. Subsequently, Ruby was assigned to a third grade class at Hayti Beverly Elementary School. The school was named after the two farmers who had owned adjoining properties before the school system acquired it, Hayes and Tilor, and the street on which it was located, Beverly. Ruby continued teaching at this elementary up to the day she retired. Beverly was dropped from the school's name in time, probably since there was another school a few miles down the street named Beverly Elementary. Romulus Community Schools closed the two story brick Hayti Elementary in June of 1988.

Earl's wife, Mickie, had given birth to their second son, Bobby Jay Etherton, called Bob, July 17, 1952. In regard to how he received the name, Bob, a commercial pilot and former Navy Pilot, noted:

> It's been a problem all my life, and even now when the TSA questions why my passport says Bobby Jay, but my airline ticket says Robert J... I tell them I cannot prevent the airline from arbitrarily changing my name

to Robert. And it all started with the nurse in Sanford, FL (where his brother was born) in 1944 and bless her heart, Mom, who bought the nurse's logic hook, line, and sinker. Ahhhh well!....

Brother Jim was born in Sanford, FL on November 1, 1944, and a nurse there told Mom that she could not name him "Jim," because it was effectively slang for either James or Jimmie. She bought that explanation and named him "Jimmie," presumably because the same nurse also considered "Jimmy" to also be an unacceptable modification of Jimmie. And so it came to be Jimmie. Fast forward 8 years to July 17, 1952, when I came along. The nurses at the Anna Hospital where I was born probably had no problem with whatever Mom wanted to name me, but she still believed what the Florida nurse had told her 8 years previously, except she did spell my name Bobby. Also, in honor of her youngest brother, Jay Givens, she gave me the middle name of Jay. Thus began my life-long name problem of "Bobby Jay..." It was cute as a little kid, but as an adult, people want to change it to Robert, and then they persist in asking me what my middle name is, to which I reply: Jay. They then come back with, "we know your initial, but what is your <u>full</u> middle name???!!! It always takes three or more of those exchanges for them to realize that I am saying the full name Jay, and not just an initial J. And it's all because of that one nurse back in Sanford, FL!!!

Ruby gave birth to the couple's third and last child, November 28, 1953, returning to Dearborn Medical Center and Dr. Castrop for the third time. Ruby and Sy decided they wanted this child to have a name starting with a J like their two other children, Judy and James. They decided on Jane Belinda or John Melvin. Ruby gave birth to a girl. When asked why the name Jane Belinda, Ruby said; "Just kind of liked the way it sounded, liked the way it went together." Jane ended up being the youngest on both sides of the family of the generation following Ruby's and Sy's.

The children of this next generation started calling each other "Cuz." The common greeting remains "Hey Cuz." It is generally believed that Jim Etherton started it, and he is certainly considered the original "Cuz." By extension, our spouses and members of the children of our generation, cousins once removed, also receive the label. At family gatherings "Cuz" is the most commonly uttered word.

Judy and I stayed with the Nichols, who had moved to Dearborn, over the weekend while Ruby was in the hospital for Jane's delivery. Judy recalls Sy picked her up Sunday night so that she could attend school the next morning. It was snowing. Judy remembers seeing the snow in the glow of the streetlights. I remained with the Nichols for a week or so. Ruby said, "Mrs. Nichols just loved you kids." Judy recalls that prior to Jane's arrival, she and a neighborhood friend, Janice Cooper, talked of the upcoming birth as if it were a big secret, complete with whispers and such. Judy figures it was a "nine-year-old girls' thing."

In the summer of 1956, Judy and I were visiting our Southern Illinois relatives. While staying with Opal and Mike Losacco on their Mount Pleasant, Illinois farm, Opal had a massive cerebral hemorrhage and died a few days later. Ruby's eldest sister died July 25, 1956, at age forty-five. I have a lasting image of her lying in her bed, barely conscious.

The teachers of Ruby's vintage were expected to dress "professionally." Rochelle Balkam, Ruby's daughter-in-law, my wife, and a long time Michigan teacher, recalls that until the late sixties female teachers were required to wear dresses or skirts, pants were strictly forbidden. In the earlier years, in addition to dresses and skirts, Ruby consistently wore nylons, high heels, and as was common at this time, a girdle. Starting in the late sixties, female teachers were allowed to wear pants suits. I remember Mother saying that they were told that the tops of their outfits must cover the "derriere" when they first were allowed to wear pants. I thought it was such a humorous expression.

Judy recalls that Mother would go shopping in mid-August and bring home several pairs of new high heel shoes to wear in the coming school year. Judy specifically remembers the boxes the shoes came in, many carried the name Baker Shoes. In contrast, Judy noted in the summer of 2010, that the teachers in the elementary school in which she teaches typically dress extremely casually. Tennis shoes and sandals are common. Dresses are rare. Some teachers even wear flip-flops when the weather is warm, even though students are not permitted to wear open toe shoes. On Fridays, most of Judy's fellow teachers wear jeans and school t-shirts or sweatshirts.

In the early years, when Ruby returned from school in the late afternoon, she would change from her rather formal attire into what she referred to as a smock, sometimes called a duster, and flat heel shoes. Unlike women today, she never wore pants.

Sy wore bib overalls, a work shirt, heavy-duty shoes, and a cap to work. Jane remembers our father donned a cap that had earflaps in the winter. He toted a lunch pail with a thermos. Ruby packed a large lunch for him each day, complete with coffee. I remember as youngsters, Judy, Jane, some times a friend or two, and I would eagerly await Dad's return from work most days. He always had a treat for us that he would dig out of that lunch pail. Jane even recalls two particular treats: a certain kind of brownie, her favorite, and fruit cocktail. Later I learned that he often stopped on his way from work at a store to make sure he had something to give us each day.

Sy returned from work with the residue of concrete and dirt on his clothes each evening. After providing us with treats, he would shed his work clothes and take a bath. Jane remembers that he would routinely call for one of us to wash his back. After his bath, Sy would put on what would now be considered a dress shirt and pants. The pants were usually sent to the commercial cleaners for cleaning. By today's standards, instead of dressing down when he got home from work, he dressed up. In the evening or on weekends, when Sy left the house he usually wore a nice fedora. Sy enjoyed stopping at a restaurant for a piece of pie, a cup of coffee, and conversation. Occasionally, he would leave his hat behind on the rack, much to Ruby's dismay.

Children in Romulus schools, until possibly the late sixties, also dressed more formally than their present day counterparts. Girls wore dresses or skirts. Sometimes high school girls wore nylons. Judy recalls occasionally, when in high school, even wearing a girdle to school. Boys wore collared shirts and nice pants, no jeans. When the school children of the day returned home in the afternoon, they changed from their school clothes into "play clothes." Whereas, Ruby remembers that male students in the country school in which she taught wore bib-overalls both during and after school.

Jane hated wearing dresses or skirts. She remembers that she was forced to do so until she started high school in the late sixties. Prior to high school, Jane could hardly wait to return home and change each day into pants, usually blue jeans or corduroys. Karen Losacco, Mikie's wife, recalls Jane would race to the nearby Losacco house to get a key to our house ahead of me, so that she could change immediately. Karen noted that I tended to lose house keys, and Ruby at a point gave up, thus leaving a key with Karen for Jane and me.

When Judy, Jane, and I were growing up, going out to eat on Friday evenings was a tradition of sorts. Judy remembers going to Howard Johnson's, located in nearby Belleville, on our birthdays. We liked the ice cream. Another place Judy remembers for their ice cream is the Daly Drive-in, particularly banana-favored ice cream. Judy figures that they must have made it themselves. It was unique and very tasty.

One of Sy's favorite places to stop for coffee and pie was the Wheel Restaurant, located about a mile or so from our Farnum Street home. The Wheel, a popular truck stop, had a sign that we thought was extremely funny. It was in the shape of a wheel with the restaurant's name in the middle and on the outer circle, which resembled a tire, on top it read "Time to Eat" and on the bottom "Gas." So when we passed that sign we would say repeatedly: "Time to eat gas" and laugh.

Jane remembers the Wheel served cream on the side in little glass containers to complement coffee. Sy would just put a little bit of the cream in his coffee, and she would get to drink the rest, licking the container to get the last drop. It got to the point that Sy would order extra cream.

In the summer, the family would travel to Detroit to see the Tigers play baseball at Briggs Stadium a few times and to Boblo Island, a popular amusement park, at least once a year. Ruby recalls that Judy, when she was very young, would have a good time playing in the bleachers in the baseball stadium. She would get extremely dirty. Ruby insisted she bathe as soon as she got home. One time, we were at a Tiger baseball game and a green parakeet landed on my shoulder. It stayed for a while, flew away, returned to my shoulder, and flew away again. The pattern was repeated a number of times. It apparently liked the bright red and white striped shirt that I was wearing, which my mother probably made. A man sitting near us suggested that we catch the little bird. Mother waited for the bird to land again, grabbed it, and put it in a paper popcorn box. We took it home, named it Tiger, put it in a cage, and it lived with us for several years.

I remember we often went to downtown Dearborn to shop. Sometimes we just looked around, window shopped, as it was called. When I was young, I had a tendency to wander off. One time while in the large Montgomery Ward Department Store in Dearborn, I did so. I was with my mother. I am not sure if anyone else was with us. Mother looked and looked. She had no idea where I was. I was probably four years of age. She alerted the management. They in turn informed their employees. An all out search ensued. One of the employees eventually found me and returned me to my mother.

To get to the amusement park on Boblo Island, a Canadian island located several miles downriver from Detroit on the Detroit River, we would travel on one of two big "steamers," the Columbia or the Ste. Claire. It was one of our favorite parts of the outing. If we were lucky Captain Boblo would be on our boat. Captain Boblo was a very small man who dressed like a boat captain. He was not the real captain. This jovial individual would interact, joke, and dance with the boat passengers, especially the children, on the trips to and from the island. He was quite the entertainer. We all liked Captain Boblo.

On one of our trips on one of the Boblo boats, I got lost once again. The boat had at least three decks. Mother, Dad, and sister Judy did their best to find me before they alerted the crew. Fortunately, Mother had Judy and me dressed in matching distinctive outfits. Mother made a lot of our clothing, including these matching pairs of shorts and tops. The crew started looking for me. A female passenger independently saw me wandering around, apparently lost. She remembered she saw a girl dressed in an outfit made of the exact same material with her parents at a particular place on the boat. She took me to that location. Fortunately, my family was there and we were reunited, thanks to a perceptive and considerate stranger.

Drive-in movies were popular in the 1950s and 1960s. Our family went to several in the summer months. When we were very young, our parents had us wear pajamas. We often fell asleep in the back seat of the car before the movie was finished. One movie I am sure I saw at a drive-in with my family and thoroughly enjoyed was the original <u>Hundred and One Dalmatians</u>. Judy recalls that the three of us children typically talked Dad into taking us directly in front of the screen to ride the little train that operated before the movie started.

It has been several years since I last saw a movie at a drive-in. I recall sitting in our parked car on a mound, which pointed the car upward in the direction of the big outdoor screen, with a portable speaker attached to one of the windows anticipating the required darkness. During the intermission, we would get out of the car and walk to the concession stand to get popcorn, candy, and soft drinks and go to the restroom. I remember the big count down clock that would periodically appear on the screen noting the time remaining in the intermission. During the movie, a truck would drive down the rows spraying a cloud of DDT, dichlorodiphenyltrichloroethane, to kill the mosquitoes.

Jane, who was a young child at the time, remembers that Mother cut her head on a cabinet in the bathroom one day. Mother stepped up onto the toilet seat with the intent of getting something out of a cabinet located above the toilet. The cabinet door was open. Mother had not seen it and hit her head on its corner. Jane recalls that there was a lot of blood. The wound was bad enough that Dad took her to the hospital. Several stitches were required to close the wound.

Jane also recalls a time when living in the Farnum Street house that a closet light fixture in the ceiling sparked a fire in the attic. Judy, who is nine years older than Jane, vividly remembers the fire. She noted that she heard the closet light bulb pop. Judy ran and got Mother. Mother took charge, got a bucket, filled it with water from the kitchen and ordered us children to go the car, shut the doors, and remain there. Independently, a man from the neighborhood saw smoke seeping from under the roof of the house and came to our aid. The fire department was called, but the fire was extinguished by the time the crew arrived at the scene.

Judy remembers seeing the firemen pulling stuff out of the attic. They determined faulty wiring caused the fire. The newly tiled floor of the bedroom she and Jane shared was damaged. It had to be replaced. Judy recalls that the floor had been covered with twelve by twelve inch pink linoleum tiles. Incidentally, the walls and curtains were also pink. Judy figures it reflected the taste of the seventh or eighth grade girl that she was at the time.

I remember Mother as being an extremely active person, rarely sitting still. She is starting to slow down just a little at age ninety-five. I understand she worked very hard at school. When she arrived home, she continued to labor until she went to bed. She cooked our meals, cleaned the house, and performed numerous house and yard related tasks. For mother's ninetieth birthday party, Jane gathered several pictures of her and made buttons for those who attended. I chose a button-depicting mother crawling from underneath our old little house with flashlight in hand while I sat on a cinder block watching her. That picture is one of my favorites and remains on my chest of drawers to this day. It reminds me how she was when I was a child. She vigorously attacked task after task be it inside, outside or for that matter, under the house.

Once our father got home, beyond a little yard work, he seemed to do very little labor. He was always supportive of my sisters and me. Among other things, it seems, he would willingly take us anywhere we wanted to go. There was always a soft spot we could find. The three of us children coined the expression "buttering up Dad" when we wanted something. Judy and I frequently would encourage the youngest, Jane, to "butter up Dad." She was particularly good at it.

Our father was by no means handy around the house. Most days, after dinner, he would go to a nearby gas station, a Gulf station, and spend a good portion of the evening talking with the employees and others who hung around the station. They called him "Pappy." I remember when Dad would refuel the car at the station, he would almost always ask the attendant for five gallons of gas. Unlike today, but common then, there was not a self-service offering.

Dad also spent a fair amount of time at a tiny store across the street from the service station. I do not remember the exact name of the store, possibly Steve's Market; we called it "Steve's" after the cigar-smoking owner. We could tell if Dad brought something home from Steve's; it reeked from the smoke of the cigar that he always seemed to have in his mouth.

It seems we would get groceries on a daily basis. There was a fruit market within two miles of our house that had a large sign on top of it depicting a pair of young people eating big pieces of watermelon along with the market's name, Van Born Fruit Market, at which we often shopped. I remember their watermelon had triangular or square plugs cut into them so that the customers could pull out the plug to view the inner melon. Additionally, it was common to thump the watermelon with a finger to determine its ripeness.

We purchased fresh chicken from the nearby Satterlee's Poultry Farm. As I recall it, a customer would view a large number of chickens and pick a favorite, then a worker would grab it, put the chicken's head facing down in a metal cone, cut off its head, let it bleed out, pluck its feather, package it, and present it to the customer. Ruby believes they might have used a wire with a hook on it to capture the chickens. The wire resembled a yard-long stretched out coat hanger. The worker would hook one of the chicken's legs and pull it in, "just like Papa did back on the farm," Ruby said.

There was a vacant field next to our house on Farnum Street that we kept mowed. I never knew who owned it. We and other kids in the neighborhood spent a lot of time playing in the field. I remember numerous pick-up baseball or softball games that took place in that field and a second field directly across the street from it. If we did not have enough players, we often played five hundred: A player earned one hundred points for catching a fly and fifty points for catching a grounder. The first person to earn five hundred points won and became the batter.

I recall putting black electrical tape around the ball once the cover was worn off. I preferred rubber coated soft or hard balls. The cover did not come off of them, and they did not get water soaked. The road and the two ditches between the two fields were interesting obstacles, but we adjusted. When I was a young boy, I remember, Mother would play softball with us. She always played in her bare feet. She said she was faster without shoes.

In the winter, we would flood the field next to our house and use it for ice-skating. I do not recall our parents ever skating with us. We would also skate on a nearby large and long drainage ditch that we called the "creek." Sometimes our parents would take us to a fire station not far from our home that had an outdoor ice rink that had lights. When we were older, we would go on our own to the rink. I believe there was no admission charge. Hot chocolate and coffee were available for a small price.

When we were children, Judy, Jane, and I would in some years spend a couple of the summer months on Uncle Wayne's farm, formerly Grover and Sarah's Union County farm, in Southern Illinois. I have several fond memories, as do Judy and Jane, of times spent on the farm. One such memory I have been reminded of several times. It was dinnertime, and I was asked to get Uncle Wayne who was working in the field near the road. I suspect I was about ten years old. I walked along the road until I was close to him. Eventually, I got his attention over the loud distinctive putt-putt sound of his large green tricycle model John Deere tractor. He turned off the engine. I yelled, "it's time for dinner." He acted as if he did not hear me. I yelled again. He cupped a hand over an ear. I yelled again. He started running toward the house and yelled; "I'll race you home." Of course, I fell for the trap and ran as fast as I could. He did have a head start and was closer to the house. Much to my dismay Uncle Wayne did, in fact, win. Upon receiving some spirited teasing from my uncle, I informed him that: "My mother would have beaten you," that is: "if she took her shoes off." In later years, Uncle Wayne loved reminding me of that story. Each time he would enthusiastically laugh, almost to tears, as he imitated me saying: "My mother would have beaten you, if she took her shoes off."

Jane believes we traveled more than was typical for families in our income bracket. We almost always made at least a trip or two a year to Southern Illinois to visit the Etherton and Owens relatives who remained there. Ruby recalls that we would sometimes leave after Sy returned from work, had bathed and changed clothes. The family would then travel as far as Indianapolis, Indiana and spend the night in a tourist home, completing the trip the following day. There was not the abundance of motels and hotels then as dots the landscape today. Tourist homes were commonly homes in which a family rented out just a room or two for the night to earn additional income.

We also traveled to Mackinac City, Niagara Falls, California and Florida. Ruby said that Sy liked to travel. All of our family trips were made in automobiles. We never flew anywhere even though we lived within a half of a mile of a major airport, Detroit Metropolitan. We did occasionally go to the airport for dinner. I was particularly fond of the large strawberry short cake that was offered at one of the restaurants. This restaurant had a view of a major runway. You could watch planes come and go as you ate.

The Mackinac Bridge opened for traffic, November 1, 1957. We made a trip to see the bridge the following summer or possibly the year after. Ruby recalls that she, Judy, Jane, and I made the five-mile trip across the bridge and back in a bus. Sy declined the opportunity. He avoided crossing large bridges, and the "Mighty Mac" is one of the largest in the world. I have crossed it several times since, and each time I avoid the outer lane as I glare straight ahead while hugging the center yellow line. Judy, Jane, and I remember playing on the windy beach under the bridge in Mackinac City that summer.

A good friend and fellow teacher of Ruby's, Callie Branham, moved to San Diego, California with her mother. She and Ruby maintained a correspondence. Callie encouraged us to visit them. Judy, Jane, and I really wanted to go to California. Judy recalls that Sy was reluctant. He said it was just too far. We pleaded. Sy eventually said that if the three of us could save $50, we would go. It took us a year or so, but we managed to save the $50. Our dad was true to his word.

In the summer of 1959 or 1960, Ruby accepted Callie's invitation, and we made the memorable cross-country trip in a white 1959 Chevrolet, the model with the large horizontal rear fins. We traveled on the famed Route 66. A song, a 1960s television series, and a movie were based on and named after this, at the time scenic, interesting, and certainly long east-west cross-country route that passed through the country side, as well as towns and cities large and small. I remember Judy, Jane, and I lobbied to stay at motels with pools each night. Jane remembers that our parents allowed each child to get some small gift in each state through which we traveled. She said I almost always chose a toy horse.

Ruby recalls that at one motel, we discovered dreaded beg bugs in the middle of the night. She said Sy, who was usually slow getting ready, was ready to go first thing this time. Ruby recalls washing all our clothing directly after arriving at Callie's house in San Diego.

Jane recalls that while approaching Needles, California, at the edge of the desert, the Chevy stopped running. It was extremely hot. Two young soldiers came to our aid. They recognized the car had a vapor lock, a common problem cars suffered in the desert. I recall that many cars traveling through the desert had cloth water filled bags hanging in front apparently to avoid vapor lock. The helpful young men had the car running in short order. Sy insisted on buying them dinner, which they gratefully accepted. Additionally, while still in the Needles area, Ruby nearly passed out. The extreme heat was too much for her.

Judy remembers at one place we stayed that a man approached us in the evening and asked if we could give him a ride. Sy and/or Ruby said no. Judy remembers as we walked into a restaurant the next morning, we saw the same man having breakfast. Sy insisted that we leave the restaurant before the man saw us.

We had a very pleasant and eventful stay in San Diego. I remember going to the world famous San Diego Zoo and seeing the big naval ships in the harbor. I recall Callie's mother had a small sports car that had great difficulty making it up some of the steep hills in San Diego. We certainly enjoyed spending time with Callie and her mother.

In the summer of 1962, the summer before Judy went off to college, we traveled to Florida. Jane recalls that we had a 1962 cordovan colored Dodge Dart. Our final destination was a motel in New Smyrna Beach, near Daytona Beach, a block from the ocean. It was the first time any of us had spent any time on an ocean beach. I remember playing continuously on the beach and in the surf on the first day. I had such a great time. I paid for it for several days. I got very ill that night and was so sun burned that I had to avoid the sun for days afterwards.

Jane recalls that it "rained like crazy" while we were in Florida. She still has a mental image of the water racing down the streets, unlike anything she had seen before and then suddenly the sun came out. Soon, it was as if it had never even rained.

A glass bottom boat tour at Silver Springs is certainly memorable. The crystal clear view of the floor of the spring fed Silver River and the colorful fish in their natural habitat was remarkable. We had never seen anything like that. One of my favorite television shows at the time was Sea Hunt, and it was filmed partially at this site, so I remember our guide saying. At the end of our boat tour, someone threw money on the big rectangular glass that we and the other tourists sat around to view the under water beauty. I reached to grab the money that I thought had been dropped, with the intent of returning it to the person who I thought must have dropped it. My embarrassed father grabbed me and explained it was intended for a tip. Sure enough, others followed suit and threw money on the glass.

The most memorable pet we had while living in the Farnum Street house certainly had to be Herman Christopher III. We called him Chris. Uncle Mike Losacco presented us three kids with this endearing registered pure brown Dachshund. A friend or possibly a tenant of Uncle Mike's, who worked for a department store, probably Sears or Montgomery Ward, decided that he could not keep this active puppy.

We kept Chris chained or on a leash while he was outside the house. Given a chance, he would run away. Chris was rather aggressive. He barked whenever anyone came to the door. I do not believe he ever bit anyone. He enjoyed running in the backyard, as his chain was hooked to either a clothesline or a stake in the ground. Chris would entertain us in the house by running and sliding on the linoleum kitchen floor. Those short legs of his seemed to move so fast. Ruby, who generally disliked having animals in the house, even grew accepting and fond of Chris.

Sy began having cerebral hemorrhages about the time Judy went off to college. Ruby suspects he had some less severe episodes previously. Each time a hemorrhage occurred he became less capable. Ruby did her best to keep him at home. Detroit Edison provided a relatively good insurance plan, but it did not cover all the incidental costs his illness entailed. It certainly did not provide money enough for this family of five to live on. Ruby had to maintain her teaching job.

There were times when Sy was hospitalized, but for the most part, he stayed at home. Ruby assumed a bulk of the care. Ruby's mother, Sarah, had started spending the winter in Michigan with our family years previously. Once Sy's illness forced him to stay home, Sarah was very good at caring for him while Ruby was at work. One time Ruby thought Aunt Mina, Sarah's younger sister, might be helpful and she was available. I recall that we traveled to Southern Illinois, picked up Sarah, rendezvoused with Aunt Mina in Carbondale, and drove back to Michigan in two cars. I spent much of the trip riding with Aunt Mina in her car. I believe that it was a compact Plymouth, maybe a Valiant. It seems she had a cigarette in her mouth the entire trip.

To this day, Ruby believes seeking aid from Aunt Mina was a big mistake. She was of little or no help. Mina and her older sister, it seemed, fought constantly. In time Aunt Mina returned to Southern Illinois, and Sarah once again assumed the care for Sy when Ruby was at school. The house was at peace again.

I have several memories of my grandmother while she stayed with us in winters on Farnum Street. She read from the Bible at least once a day, and she did not do so silently. Grandma often told us we should begin reading the Bible on a daily basis. She suggested a half hour to an hour each day. She would regularly tell us what Billy Graham had noted in his daily article. There was a church in Wayne, Michigan that she often attended. Ruby and Sy, when he was healthy enough, would drive Sarah and Judy, Jane, and me to the church, drop us off, and pick us up after church was done. Ruby and Sy never attended church with us. Judy, once she was old enough, would drive us to church.

I remember one time Grandma, Mother, Jane, and I were shopping at a Montgomery Wards Department Store, and Grandmother, Jane, and I had our picture taken with a new type of camera. The photographer snapped our picture, pulled it out of the camera, and we watched our black and white image develop on the spot. We had never seen the likes of that before. It was the launching of what became the popular Polaroid Instant Camera.

Sarah visibly enjoyed getting out and seeing different things while she wintered with us. Suburban Detroit was considerably different from her Southern Illinois home. We took her to hockey games, shopping in large stores, and special events. One such event that she particularly enjoyed was a Donkey Basketball game at Romulus High School. She laughed almost uncontrollably.

Ruby recalls coming home from school, talking with her mother as Sarah complained of being tired, but perked up immediately once Ruby suggested that we eat out. Sarah would jump off the couch, get her coat out of the closet, put on her coat, and impatiently wait for Ruby and the rest of us to get ready.

Television certainly became a source of entertainment for Sarah while in Michigan. It seemed to be somewhat of a contradiction that she enjoyed "soap operas" as much as she did. She referred to them as her stories. I remember coming home from school, being told what Billy Graham's advice of the day was, and then receiving updates on shows such as the Guiding Light, All My Children, and As the World Turns. I remember her telling me the sordid and sometimes crude details. Whereas, she would have a fit if someone swore or used a word like sex in her presence. I have seen her assertively announce to strangers that she did not approve of their language.

I have an image of Grandma going outside on a snowy day and playing with us. She must have been in her late seventies. She wore a pair of Dad's bib-overalls. I remember pulling her on a sled and seeing her tip over into the snow. She laughed and laughed as she lay in the snow.

In the winter, one of the family's favorite things to do was to make "snow ice cream." Ruby recalls she would get the three of us children to gather clean white snow; mix it with milk, a raw egg, vanilla, sugar, and sometimes nutmeg in a big blue and white two-toned bowl. Jane still has and uses this bowl. It is blue on the outside and white on the inside. After Ruby vigorously beat up this cold mixture, we ate it quickly for it melted very rapidly.

7 *Death of Husband*
Age 47 to Age 62

After graduating from Romulus High School, Judy moved to Goodison Hall on Eastern Michigan University's campus in the fall of 1962. I recall visiting Judy with my parents. I liked it when we stopped at Miller's Ice Cream Shop, which featured hand dipped ice cream. This old-fashioned ice cream shop was located on Michigan Avenue on the east side of Ypsilanti.

I remember going to homecoming with my older sister one time. Eastern's football team was so bad that one of the speakers at half time said the EMU receivers and backs needed to put chewing gum on their hands so they might hang onto the football.

Judy married Robert Bruce Leonard, typically called Bob, March 27, 1964, in a Congregational Church in nearby Wayne, Michigan. It was Ruby's forty-ninth birthday. Sy was fifty-nine and was very weak and ill. He insisted on walking Judy down the church aisle. Ruby and others thought he might not be able to do so. Sy persisted and pulled it off.

Robert Leonard resided in several states as a child. His daughter, Jennifer Leonard Samborski, recalls her father telling her that he had attended as many as forty-nine or fifty different schools from kindergarten through high school. While serving in the army, Bob befriended a Michigan native, Larry Wade. After leaving the army, Bob returned to his birthplace, San Francisco, California to attend college. He decided almost immediately that college was not the place for him. He no longer wanted to be told what to do.

An army buddy of Bob and Larry's was going to get married. He wanted to invite Larry to the wedding; Larry was not responding to letters or calls. Bob decided he would find Larry, find out if anything was wrong and relay the invitation. Bob did have an address. He had very little money. A determined Bob set out for this long cross-country trip by train, hopping on freight trains. The trip took a very long time. Jennifer does not know exactly how long. She does remember him telling her of several delays and encounters along the way. She recalls, for instance, that he stopped in Las Vegas and tested out being a professional gambler. It quickly became obvious that it was not for him.

Having little money for even lodging and food, Bob learned that if he showed up at a town jail by 5 p.m. that he could get a free dinner, breakfast, and a bed for the night before they escorted him out of town the next morning. After completing the trip to Michigan, Bob did find Larry and learned that he had cancer. Larry did survive. He and Bob regrettably never made it to their friend's wedding. Bob remained in the area and secured a job at Jim Davis Chevrolet in Wayne, Michigan as a mechanic and developed a friendship with Wayne Pendley.

Judy and her two best friends, Diane Barker and Alberta Sayger, triple dated Wayne, Bob, and a third young man. In time Wayne and Diane married, as did Bob and Judy. It did not work out with Alberta and the third man. Instead, she ended up marrying Wayne's older brother Art.

One time Chris, the active family dog, lost control as he was running and sliding through the kitchen. He slipped a disk; apparently older Dachshunds commonly do so. Bob Leonard built a cart with attaching straps and two rear wheels. Chris, in time, learned to navigate the cart rather well using just his front paws. After a couple of months, Chris recovered and lived for several years, although he walked rather awkwardly and rarely really ran again.

Sy, at age sixty, died from pneumonia after numerous cerebral hemorrhages and Parkinson's disease weakened both his body and mind. He died July 1st, 1965, the day before my sixteenth birthday. Two of the last things Sy told Ruby were: "Take care of the kids." and "You should get out of here." He meant that we should move from our little old house on Farnum Street.

There were two funeral services held for Sy, one at a funeral home in neighboring Wayne, Michigan and a second at the gravesite in the

Harrisburg, Illinois area. A friend of Sy's, who spent a lot of time at the gas station with him, insisted on driving Ruby, Jane and me from Michigan to Southern Illinois. Elmer Miller, almost always called Miller, drove us to Harrisburg then made the return trip by bus. In this difficult time, we certainly appreciated Miller's numerous entertaining stories on the ride to Southern Illinois. He initially refused to accept any money, not even to cover return bus fare. Ruby eventually talked the reluctant Miller into letting her pay the bus fare, noting that a collection from the neighbors was intended for such. Judy and Bob drove separately.

Sy was born on a farm a few miles outside of Harrisburg. The family moved to the city when he was young, before he started school. Sy's father, McClellan, typically called Clell or Uncle Clell, got a job as a truant officer for the Harrisburg schools. He had an old truck that he used to search for, find, and transport truant students to school. In time, Clell became a custodian at one of the schools. Ruby does not recall when the job change took place.

At some point, Clell became acquainted with a local mobster of note, Charlie Birger. A book published in 1952 by Paul M. Angle entitled Bloody Williamson features the Birger gang, the rival Shelton Brother's gang, the Ku Klux Klan, and local law enforcement. In a Wikipedia entry, it was noted that Charlie Birger was the last man executed in a public hanging in the state of Illinois, April 19, 1928. It was also noted that many local public officials might very well have profited from Birger's bootlegging activities. The local mobster apparently liked "Uncle Clell" a lot and put the word out that "no one was to mess with that old man," according to Ruby. She also noted that public officials commonly used Clell to communicate with Birger and vise versa. The nature of the communication is not known. Jane recalls hearing Bob Rose, a long time Harrisburg resident and a cousin by marriage, talk about this connection between Charlie Birger and "Uncle Clell."

Clell donated part of the family farm to a local church, Social Brethren Church, and was allocated several choice plots in its adjoining Spring Valley Cemetery. Sy was born at the top of one hill on the Owens family farm, and sixty years later family and friends gathered to bury him on an adjacent hill in Spring Valley Cemetery.

A few weeks after Sy's death, as I was backing a car into the garage, my mother walked out of the front door, met me in the driveway and in a somber tone told me that Sue Etherton had been killed. Sue was Wayne's, Ruby's eldest brother, second child. She was only eighteen. She was riding home with friends late at night on the Dongola Road within a few miles of the family farm. The driver lost control of the car. The vehicle ran off the road and rolled over several times down a hill. She was the only one in the car to perish. Sue's unexpected death was certainly a shock.

Just before Sy became ill, he had hired someone to paint the Farnum Street house green. Ruby never did like the color. A few weeks after the funeral, she and I scraped and painted the house. Ruby believes we painted it white. I do not remember.

Ruby sold "our little old house" near the end of 1965, and we moved to a new subdivision about a mile away. It was the last available three-bedroom house in the subdivision. We remained in the same school district, so Jane and I were able to graduate from Romulus High, just as Judy had done. Ruby now lived just about a mile from Hayti, where she continued to teach.

Sy's illnesses had drained the family's savings; Ruby had just enough left to pay his funeral expenses. She disliked having debt of any kind, but it certainly was not as troublesome to Sy. He did not mind buying things on credit and making payments.

I recalled my father loved to look at cars both new and used. At the time, the American Automobile Companies came out with new models with great fanfare every year. I remember in the fall regularly seeing cloth covered cars stacked both on trains and truck car-carriers. The car dealers' windows were covered, be it with existing shades or large pieces of paper. On a designated fall day preceding the coming new-year, the covers were taken off, the shades were open, and the paper was removed. We, like many others, would make the rounds to see the new offerings by General Motors, Ford, Chrysler, and American Motors.

We purchased and traded in cars relatively often. Dad always seemed to be in the market for a different car. It was not uncommon for him to appear in the driveway with a car that he was test-driving. He did not shy away from making payments. Ruby preferred to pay cash for everything, if at all possible.

Ruby applied the total proceeds from the sale of the Farnum Street house to the cost of the new house. Once things stabilized, the fifty-year old Ruby began making larger than required payments and managed to pay for the new house in short order. Cousin Mikie Losacco is fairly certain the house was priced at $12,990 in 1965.

Mikie and his family had moved to the same new subdivision a few months earlier. Mikie, Karen, and three young children, Steven, Greg, and Doreen had lived in the Chicago area previously. Karen had been born and raised in Chicago. Karen gave birth to a fourth child, Richard Wayne Losacco, normally called Ricky, a couple of years after they moved to Michigan. We certainly enjoyed living near our cousins. Additionally, Ruby noted that she was "glad to get out of that old house. It was a good move for me."

This new house was on Niagara Street in Romulus behind a set of apartment buildings. The children in the neighborhood attended Hayti Elementary School. Ruby had a number of them in either fourth or second grade, including three of the Losacco children. Doreen never had Ruby as a teacher, but each of the three boys did. The Losacco children avoided addressing Ruby as Aunt Ruby while at school. Ruby said they just looked at her when they talked to her and did not call her anything. Mikie, Karen, Ruby, and the Losacco children had talked about this at home and had decided on this approach.

There were several people who were particularly supportive of our family after Sy's death. In addition to relatives, there were two notable individuals--Ben Robbins and Elmer Miller. Ben was the custodian at Hayti Elementary School and served as a constable for Romulus Township. After Sy's death and our move to the Niagara Street house, Ben, who patrolled the new neighborhood in the evenings, would routinely shine a spot-light in our window as he passed the house. He wanted us to know that he was looking out for us. At school, when cars were covered with snow and/or ice, Ben would often brush the snow off Ruby's car and scrape off the ice.

Miller, Sy's good friend, would occasionally stop by the house to see how we were doing, and to see if he could do anything to help out. Soon after moving into our new house, Ruby had a two and a half car garage built. She liked keeping her car in a garage especially in the

71

winter. She preferred to avoid the need to remove snow and ice from the car windows during Michigan's cold winter mornings.

Miller restored vintage automobiles. For several years, Miller kept a beautifully restored 1928 Chevrolet in our garage. It was painted a shiny dark green with black fenders. Whenever friends or family visited, we had to show them the car. Miller would occasionally take one or two of us for a ride. There was only room for three in its single seat. I remember people in passing cars would take extra long looks at us as we putt-putted along. Jane arranged to have Miller drive his classic car in a Romulus High School Homecoming Parade, representing the National Honor Society of which Jane was a member. The witty Miller and his car were a big hit.

After we moved to the house on Niagara, a good friend of Ruby's and her husband moved into the adjacent apartment complex. Mae Cole worked with Ruby in the Romulus School District. Much of the time, she worked as a visiting teacher, serving students who were unable to attend school. Mae's husband Clarence, called Dub, was a quiet man and loved to fish. Mae and Dub would invite our family to spend time with them at their cottages "up north" a few times a year. The first cottage was on Cedar Lake near the town of Oscoda. The second was on Grand Lake near Alpena. Dub taught me how to fish. He and I would spend hours at a time in a rowboat and hardly utter a word as we each waited to feel a bite on our fishing lines.

Mae developed cancer. She had no family in the area. She moved to an apartment near our house so she could be close to Ruby. Ruby did what she could to help out. Mae died a short time after the move. Dub moved in with his daughter soon afterwards. He became very ill and lived only a couple of years after Mae's death.

Ruby decided to get a master's degree. It would mean a salary increase. She began taking evening and summer masters level classes. Jane fondly remembers taking a typing class one summer at Ypsilanti High School, while her mother was taking a class at Eastern Michigan University. Ruby said she wanted Jane to have something constructive to do, while she was taking classes. Romulus High School did apply credit for the typing class to Jane's high school record. Ruby proudly completed the required courses in the summer of 1967 and was awarded a Master of Arts degree in August. I graduated from high school the previous June and enrolled at Eastern.

The 1967 Detroit riots started in the early morning hours on Sunday, July 23, after the police raided an unlicensed after hours bar, a "blind pig." The author of a Wikipedia entry noted that it was " . . . one of the deadliest and most destructive riots in American history, lasting five days and surpassing the violence and destruction of Detroit's 1943 race riot." George Romney, the governor at the time, sent in the National Guard and President Lyndon B. Johnson sent in Army troops. Forty-three people were killed, four hundred sixty-seven were injured, more than seven thousand were arrested, and more than two thousand buildings were destroyed.

Detroit and its suburbs were put under a tight dusk to dawn curfew. Bob Leonard was working in Detroit at the time at a tire dealer. Judy remembers he was permitted to be out during curfew hours, as he traveled to and from work, but was stopped occasionally and had to verify his need to be out during the curfew.

This was the summer after I graduated from high school. I worked at a gas station, Tulsa Oil in Westland, Michigan. There were only two of us attendants who agreed to work during the riots. The station stayed open for only seven or eight hours a day. We were prohibited from putting gasoline in portable containers. Several customers were angered by this and often noted; they just wanted to mow their lawns. Our work was nonstop, the entire time we were open. I remember people telling me they were getting away from the area. You could see the smoke from the burning Detroit buildings from where we worked and lived.

Judy gave birth to Ruby's first grandchild, July 17, 1968. Judy and Bob named their child Robert Bruce Leonard, Junior. We called him Rob. The summer of Rob's birth was another difficult summer for the country. Martin Luther King, Junior was assassinated on April 4th and Robert F. Kennedy on June 5th. Judy recalls that our area was once again put under a curfew.

Ruby remembers traveling to Southern Illinois with her younger sister Florence in the early 1970s. Florence complained of pain near her eye. Ruby observed a large red spot. She told her sister she needed to see a doctor. After they returned to Michigan, Ruby accompanied

Florence to a medical facility. She had cancer in her head, behind an eye. Florence had the eye removed along with a sizeable portion of her face. She suffered a great deal. Ruby believes Florence died three or four years after the initial diagnosis. The casket was closed at the funeral. She died November 8, 1976 at age 54.

Ruby was Florence's primary caregiver during this difficult time. A couple of years into the illness, Florence worried that she might lose her house. Ruby suggested that her sister transfer the deed to the house to her. Ruby guaranteed she would not lose it. After Florence died, twenty-two year old Jane stayed in the house for several weeks, so it would not stand vacant, sleeping on a mattress on the floor. Jane recalls that Mikie and Karen Losacco helped her and Ruby paint the interior walls. Ruby sold the house soon afterwards. With the proceeds, she paid Florence's funeral bill and related expenses. The remaining money was turned over to Florence's only child, Ronnie, as Florence requested.

Jane graduated from Romulus High School, June of 1971. She started attending Michigan Technological University in September and graduated four years later with a degree in biological sciences. She remained an additional year and earned a second Bachelor of Science Degree. This degree was in Medical Technology.

Mother, Judy, and I had all attended Eastern Michigan University. Jane instead chose Michigan Tech, as it is called, which is located nearly six hundred miles away from Romulus. Ruby fondly recalls the trip in August of 1971 in which she and Mrs. Hayes, a friend of Ruby's and one of Jane's best friend's mother, took the new freshman to Michigan Tech for orientation. Ruby said she enjoyed the trip to and from, but Jane did not want her mother to stay any longer than was necessary. Jane was eager to get started in this new phase of her life.

I earned my bachelor's degree from Eastern Michigan in August and joined the Peace Corps in October of 1971. I served two years teaching secondary mathematics in a village of about eight thousand people, Mochudi, Botswana.

When I left for Botswana in the fall of 1971, Ruby was alone in the Niagara Street house. The Losaccos fortunately were within a block, she had developed friendships with neighbors, and Judy and Bob lived in the area. Jane returned to Romulus on school vacations. Ruby wrote to me weekly. We did not talk via telephone at all while I stayed in the distant African village.

Ruby continued to travel after Sy's death. Jane recalls traveling with Ruby to Ocean City, Maryland either while she was in high school or during the early years of college. She recalls an image of the two of them walking on the Atlantic Ocean beach. After Jane's second year in college, in the summer of 1972, she and Ruby traveled to the Bahamas. It was the first time either of them had traveled off the continent. They had traveled to nearby Canada a number of times, including a few trips to Algoma Mills, Ontario. Opal and Mike Losacco's eldest, Jenny, had married Michael Pinto, the Chief Operations Officer of a large Detroit area engineering company, Pioneer Engineering. Mike and Jenny Pinto owned a private lodge ninety miles east of Sault Saint Marie. Our family enjoyed spending a week or so in the summers at the Pinto lodge, located on the crystal clear Lake Lauzon.

The Pintos employed a caretaker at the "lodge." His name was Mr. Pelki and he had a pet crow named Pete. I have fond memories of Mr. Pelki. One time he and I were getting a boat ready to go out on the lake. We were determining if there was enough gas in the boat's tank. He started to take off the cap to look into the tank. I said something, like why don't you look at the gauge, which was clearly visible. His evasive expression told me he could not read the gauge. Later observations confirmed that the elder man could not read. I regretted my earlier expression. We all liked Mr. Pelki a great deal.

Pete the crow could in fact utter a few words. He would usually accompany us when we went fishing, especially if Mr. Pelki was with us. It was hardly quiet when Pete was around. He would fly around the boat uttering the few words he knew and generally being raucous, as crows are. Pete was extremely playful. Friends of the Pintos, the Andersons, would often visit the lodge on the same week of the year as we did. Two of the Anderson children were close in age to Jane and me. They had a big friendly Labrador retriever. Pete drove the dog crazy. I have this lasting memory of Pete teasing the lab, the lab aggressively chasing Pete, Pete flying low, staying just a little ahead of the pursuing barking dog, leading it onto the dock, the dog within inches of the crow. The playful bird led the lab right off the end of the dock. It seemed the dog had no sense of what was happening as it splashed into the cold clear lake. Pete circled and seemed to laugh at the lab as he swam to the shore.

Ruby's second grandchild and first granddaughter was born December 9, 1973. Judy and Bob named their second child Jennifer Ann Leonard. Judy recalls that Jennifer was afraid of me when she was very young. Judy figures it was because of the beard and long hair I had at the time.

Ruby fondly recalls a trip she made with Rob, Judy's eldest child, when he was five or six years old. The trip occurred in mid-June at the beginning of her summer vacation. Ruby and Rob traveled to Southern Illinois. Rob loved looking at and reading maps; literally wearing them out in short order. He was also very capable, even at this young age, so much so that Ruby had faith in her little navigator. On this particular trip, Rob wanted to see downtown Indianapolis. Thus, in Ruby words, "He really tricked me." As soon as she made a particular turn, she realized it but decided to go along with it, and they traveled through downtown Indianapolis. She still recalls how pleased he was with himself as he sat in the backseat, which was cluttered with maps and books.

8 Family Deaths
Age 62 to Age 87

Sarah came to the Niagara Street house in Romulus in the fall of 1977, intending to spend another winter in Michigan. She became ill and insisted on returning to Southern Illinois. Ruby said her mother wanted to die at home. Lillian Etherton, a registered nurse and Sarah's daughter-in-law, oversaw Sarah's care. She suffered from "heart trouble" and developed pneumonia. Sarah died in a Southern Illinois hospital, January 9th, just one month shy of her ninety-fourth birthday. She was born near the Little Wabash River in Southern Illinois, February 10, 1884, about seventy-five miles from that hospital.

Ruby traveled to Southern Illinois to spend time with her mother, December 17, 1977. She returned to Michigan on the twenty-second and continued preparing to move to a new home. She recalls her mother saying, "I'll never be able to see your new house."

Ruby had found a pleasant ranch style house on Grandon Street in nearby Livonia. She particularly liked the location of the house. It was located within walking distance of Wonderland Shopping Mall and the credit union of which Ruby was a member.

It was an extremely cold December day in 1977, when we moved Ruby to the new house. Judy's husband, Bob Leonard, described the move in his daily journal:

> The day after Christmas has been bitterly cold. A light
> wind made it worse and the fact that we had to be out
> all day didn't help.

> We started out to move Ruby today. Nothing but trouble. First, Jim couldn't get the truck he wanted. The one he did get quit running before it reached Ruby's. We went back to get another truck and it wouldn't start. We finally got it going and were able to move Ruby in two loads.
>
> Somewhere along the line, Jim lost the contract on the truck. So Judy is going to have to argue for the deposit.

I suspect Judy did secure the deposit. Neither of us can remember for sure. I do recall that the stalled U-Haul truck remained on the side of the road near our former home for several days before being retrieved.

Two and half years after the move to Livonia, the sixty-five year old Ruby retired from teaching in June of 1980. She had worked for Romulus Community Schools for thirty-one years in addition to the five years in one-room schools in Southern Illinois. In Romulus, Ruby had worked at three different elementary schools. In her first year, she spent half the school day at Airport Elementary and half at Texas Elementary. The next two years were spent full-time at Airport Elementary followed by twenty-eight years at Hayti Elementary.

She had worked with seven different principals. Prior to Ruby's retirement, The Enterprise Roman, the local newspaper, printed an invitation to an open house honoring her. The article included a brief history of her teaching career and a salute. The closing paragraph noted, "Mrs. Owens has been an inspiration to her students and fellow teachers during her many fine years of teaching."

The Board of Education passed a resolution of congratulations in which it was noted, " . . . she has made many contributions to the education profession and has touched the lives of countless students during her tenure at Romulus Community School."

Jane married a fellow Michigan Tech graduate, Daniel Mathena, in August of 1978. Jane recalls Ruby often traveled with her and Dan when they went on vacation. On one trip, Jane and Daniel drove and Ruby flew to Jackson Hole, Wyoming. In addition, Jane remembers traveling in the couple's "little Datsun truck" and visiting several national parks. Jane and Dan would sleep in a small tent, and Ruby would sleep in the back of the truck.

Tara Mathena, Ruby's third and last grandchild, was born November 30, 1984. When Tara was eighteen months old, Jane, Dan, Ruby, and Tara traveled to Yellowstone National Park and Lake Louise in a Toyota van. Jane noted, "I got food poisoning really bad, and it was a good thing Mother was along to take care of Tara while Daniel drove."

I married Rochelle Balkam, October 21, 1981. She and I met soon after I started teaching in the Ypsilanti district. I taught mathematics; she taught history. Rochelle recalls that soon after we started dating in May of 1979, I invited her to accompany me as I took Mother out to dinner for Mother's Day. Rochelle has said repeatedly since that she knew I was serious at that point.

Ruby's three children remained relatively near their mother geographically. Rochelle and I settled about thirty miles away in Ann Arbor. Jane and Tara lived in nearby Canton, about ten miles away. Jane and Dan were divorced in June of 1988. Judy and her family ended up in neighboring Garden City, within a couple of miles of Ruby's house.

Several years after Ruby retired from teaching, she joined the Livonia Travel Club. With the club, she traveled to numerous sites within the state, the country, and Canada. On one memorable trip, brother Wayne and his wife Lillian accompanied Ruby to Alaska. Ruby said Wayne really enjoyed the trip, seeing glaciers and other beautiful natural land, water, and ice formations.

Through Ruby's involvement with the travel club, she developed a close friendship with Leona Fortune. Leona served as the president of the club, and Ruby was her assistant. Most members in the club were retirees. Ruby said, "Some of the members were worse than kids." Many an argument developed over the choice of bus seats. On multiple day trips, seats were rotated to insure fairness and minimize confrontations. Ruby said trips to casinos were always fully booked. She had no interest in traveling to the casinos.

Ruby's interest in art was rekindled. This proclivity began while in high school in Herrin, Illinois, primarily using colored chalk, pastels.

Rochelle and I have our favorite picture of hers, which is of this vintage, proudly hanging in our bedroom. It pictures an attractive spring running through lush green woods.

While teaching in one-room schools, she painted several natural scenes depicting her rural environment with watercolors and oils. She remembers encouraging her students to draw and paint, recalling that there were a few who demonstrated innate talent. As we spoke, she expressed great pleasure in the fact that she exposed these students of rural Southern Illinois to art.

Soon after retiring, Ruby took an art class, which focused on oil painting. Her instructor, Muriel, lived in the vicinity and held class in her basement. Judy recalls that she and husband Bob went to at least one exhibit featuring Muriel's students' works including a number of Ruby's paintings. Ruby remembers that Muriel moved away to Wisconsin.

Ruby continued producing numerous oil paintings for several years, some of which reflected images of her childhood life on the farm. Other paintings were of scenes from her travels such as the unique emerald colored Lake Louise with a glacier in the background.

She also took classes offered by the Singer Sewing Machine Company at Wonderland Mall. One class focused on needlepoint. In a corner of the living room of our Ann Arbor home, Rochelle and I have a photograph of the rondoval I lived in while in Mochudi, Botswana on one wall and the needlepoint patterned on the photograph vaguely appearing to be a reflection on the adjoining wall.

Judy has two needlepoints on display at her Garden City home. Both are winter scenes: One of an owl positioned on a branch and the second of a pair of geese in flight in a snow sprinkled sky.

Ruby's sister Mary was diagnosed with a severe form of cancer in 1988. Uncle Jim told the family that the doctors indicated she would live ten years at most. Over the next several years, Ruby traveled numerous times to Marion, Illinois to be at her younger sister's side. Judy recalls driving with Ruby a number of times to Marion and returning on the train. On other occasions, Ruby would catch a flight from Detroit Metropolitan Airport to St. Louis then to the small airport in Marion. She would often remain in Marion up to a couple of months at a time.

Judy remembers that during one visit, Jim Fox had a heart attack.

Judy took him to the local hospital. They then transferred him to a Springfield hospital directly, transporting him in an ambulance. Judy stayed in Springfield for several days then returned to Michigan to care for her children. Ruby stayed in Springfield until Jim was released.

Mary Fox, Ruby's last surviving sister, died on June 9th of 1996. She was seventy-seven. The doctors aggressively fought the cancer, and Mary's quality of life was pretty good until the last two years of her life. Ruby said, "Near the end, Mary did not want me out of her sight. I slept on the floor next to her bed."

Ruby's eldest sibling, Wayne, died of natural causes, a little more than a year after Mary's death, Aug. 29, 1997. Wayne was eighty-eight years of age, having been born March 8, 1909.

A couple of years after Wayne's death, Lillian traveled with Ruby on a tour through the Panama Canal. A somewhat frail Lillian lost her balance while on an escalator. A well-intentioned man grabbed her as she was falling, resulting in a broken rib.

On November 22, 1998, a second rollover automobile accident tragically claimed the life of a second young family member, Ricky Losacco. Ricky, the youngest of Mikie and Karen's children, Ruby's nephew, was thirty-one years of age. Wayne and Lillian's youngest child, Sue, had died in a rollover accident in 1965 at age eighteen.

The year 2002 was a particularly harsh one for Ruby's extended family. Earl Etherton, Ruby's youngest brother, died of natural causes, October 1, 2002. He was eighty-five years of age. Ruby, the fourth oldest of eight children, now was the sole surviving child of Sarah and Grover Etherton. Lillian Etherton, Ruby's eldest brother's wife, died of natural causes November 9, 2002. Lillian was ninety-one. Jim Fox, Mary's husband, Mickie Etherton, Earl's wife, and Ruby were now the last members of their generation. Jim was eighty-six, Mickie was eighty, and Ruby was the oldest at eighty-seven years of age.

Jim Etherton graduated from Dongola High School in 1961. In November of 1973, he bought his alma mater and began the long process of converting it to a residence complete with a music studio. The small high school had eight classrooms, a full basement, a full size gym and big tubular fire escapes on two sides of the building from the second floor to the ground.

In November of 1999 and 2002, many of the Etherton relatives gathered at Jim Etherton's Dongola, Southern Illinois home to celebrate Thanksgiving with a reunion. Most of the Michigan relatives made the trip south each time. Judy and her family missed the second of the two gatherings. The Etherton relatives had a grand time at each gathering. There was abundant reminiscing, a large variety of good food, and lively entertainment. Jim Etherton, the original Cuz, served as the piano man. Ronnie Casmer, Bob and Bill Etherton and David Samborski played a variety of guitars. There were local guests playing drums, guitars, and sharing vocals with the Etherton musicians.

In 2002, the day after Thanksgiving, tragedy struck. In the evening, word was received that Rob Leonard, Judy's son and Ruby's first grandchild, had died of a massive heart attack. Rob and his father were returning from the Chrysler Museum in Auburn Hills, Michigan. Fortunately Bob was driving. Bob got his son to a hospital as soon as he could. Robert Leonard, Jr. died on November 29, 2002 at age thirty-four.

9 The Last of a Generation
Age 90 to 97

Family and friends marked Ruby's ninetieth birthday at the Dearborn Inn with brunch in March of 2005. Her nephew Bill Etherton and his wife Judy, who reside in Dongola, Illinois, traveled the furthest. Four or five of Ruby's former colleagues from Hayti Elementary attended. People, who had not seen her in recent years, as well as the staff at the Dearborn Inn, noted how youthful she appeared.

After the ninetieth celebration, Ruby's birthday became an annual family event for her Michigan relatives with gatherings at Buca De Beppa in Livonia and Station 885 in Plymouth. The celebration was again expanded to include more relatives, friends, and former colleagues to mark her ninety-fifth birthday at Station 885 in Plymouth. Bill and Judy Etherton from Southern Illinois attended again. They say they will also make it to her hundredth celebration. Jim Etherton from Dongola, Bob and Georgette Etherton from Germantown, Tennessee also made the trip north.

Ruby, who is happiest when she is busy, put forth considerable effort and obtained apparent pleasure and pride in the canning of tomatoes and applesauce each fall. During the summer, she often declared how much she looked forward to canning in the fall. She typically canned three bushels of tomatoes in quart jars, as many as 50 quarts a year. She canned an equal number of containers of applesauce, some in pint jars and some in quarts. The applesauce was exclusively made from empire apples with candy red-hots added for flavor. At Christmas, Ruby routinely gave each of her Michigan relatives a collection of canned goods. Judy, Jane, and I typically received twelve quarts of tomatoes and twelve containers of applesauce.

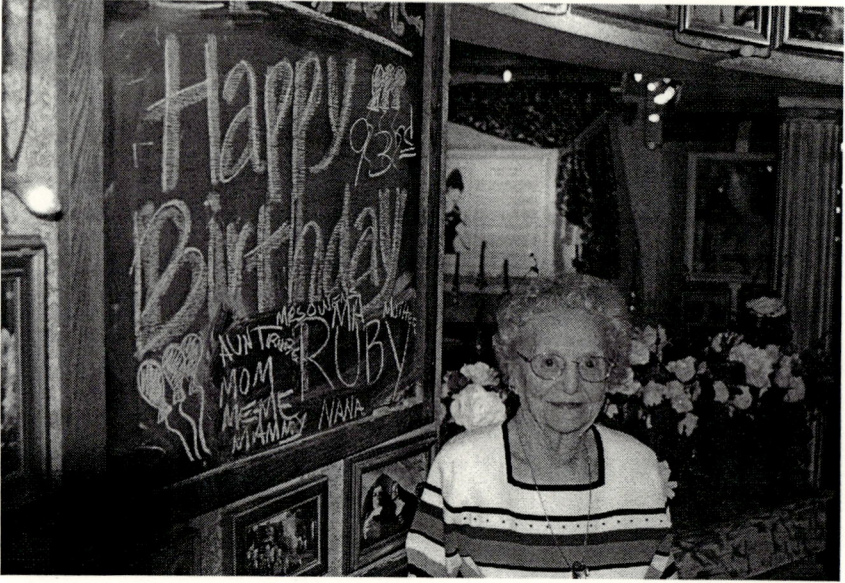

Ruby's 93rd birthday celebration

Ruby continued canning up to age 95. That last year her two granddaughters Jennifer and Tara, and great grandson Levi helped. I remember Mother talking about how much fun the 6-year-old Levi had. According to Ruby, his hands were just the correct size for stuffing the tomatoes into the jars.

Dr. Lewis, Ruby's primary physician, credits her good health to good genes and exercise. Immediately after retiring from teaching, Ruby began walking for exercise. Until nearby Wonderland Mall was closed, she would walk a little more than a mile to the mall, walk three times around a one and a quarter mile course, and then walk back home. The walk took about an hour and a half; she typically walked five days a week.

According to the website www.deadmalls.com, "The whole mall (Wonderland) was shuttered in 2003." After the closing, Ruby started walking in her neighborhood, developing a 2.2-mile course. She continued to regularly walk for exercise up to age 94 or possibly even 95.

Until around age 96, Ruby's preferred sitting position was on the floor with legs folded under her body, essentially sitting on her ankles. Several much younger people after witnessing Ruby have tried to replicate this distinctive seating posture, few succeeded. Even fewer were able to stand straight up from the floor without any assistance and without grabbing onto anything as Ruby did.

Ruby's favorite sitting position,
Gravestone for the two children that died at birth

In December of 2008, Ruby at age 93 became the sole surviving member of her generation in the family. Her brother-in-law Jim Fox died November 7th and her sister-in-law Mickie Etherton died December 12th. Jim was ninety-two and a half, and Mickie was eighty-six years of age.

Ruby booked two memorable trips to Mackinac Island through the Livonia Travel Club, one in October of 2005 and the other in September of 2009. On the first trip, Ruby and daughter Judy traveled with a group on a charter bus, meeting Barbara Fortune on the island. Barbara was the daughter of Ruby's late friend, Leona Fortune, former president of the Livonia Travel Club. Jane joined them on the second trip. All reported having an enjoyable time.

Each time they stayed at the beautiful and historic Grand Hotel. The Grand received its first guests in 1887. The foursome spent a lot of time sitting on the large front porch, which offers a great panoramic view of the Straits of Mackinac and the five-mile long Mackinac Bridge.

Tourists not staying at the hotel are charged ten dollars for the privilege of walking onto the Grand's porch.

Automobiles are not allowed on the island. Jane, Judy, and Ruby remember walking a great deal. Judy and Jane remember circling the island on bicycles, an eight-mile trip. The group rode in horse drawn taxis and went on carriage tours of the island.

Jane noted she and Barbara swam in the hotel swimming pool, even though it was "freezing cold." The group took a jewelry class, went on a tour of the extremely large and bustling kitchen, and had impressive multiple course dinners at the Grand.

Ruby continues to live on her own in her Livonia home. She is now 97. The year is 2012. Her daughters, Judy and Jane, stop by most days and have assumed more and more responsibility. I take her out to lunch once a week or so.

It is notable how healthy and active she remains. She likes to tell of the time an aide to her doctor told her that she, the aide, wished she had Ruby's blood. Ruby is still able to work in the yard in the spring and summer. In the fall, she obsessively keeps her yard clear of leaves.

Abigale Samborski, Judy's first grandchild, interviewed her great-grandmother for a project in second grade. Ruby was ninety-four years of age at the time. Abigale's interview reflects how dramatically life has changed over the course of Ruby's many years. The questions were typed out by the teacher and Abigale wrote out the answers based on her great grandmother's responses.

Question: "How did you get to your elementary school? About how far away was your school from your home?"

Answer: "She walked one mile to school."

Question: "How did you dress for school in the summer and in the winter?"

Answer: "She wore dresses all the time."

Question: "What did you do after school?"

Answer: "She had to gather eggs, bring in wood, and help cook."

Question: "About how many channels did you get on your television?"

Answer: "She had no TV, phones, or radio."

Question: "At what restaurants did your family eat when you were a child?"

Answer: "There were no restaurants where she lived."

Question: "What kind of pet(s) did you have when you were a child? What did you feed it (them)."

Answer: "She did not have any but her brother had dogs. The dogs ate scraps."

Question: "How did you make popcorn?"

Answer: "She used a skillet."

Question: "How did your family heat your home?"

Answer: "They cut wood and put it in the stove."

Question: "Did your family have air conditioning? How did your family cool the house in the hot summertime?"

Answer: "They did not have air conditioning so they went under a shade tree."

Question: "What kind of car(s) did your parents drive?"

Answer: "They had no cars. They used wagons."

Question: "What were the names of the grocery stores, clothing stores, drug stores, and hardware stores to which your family went when you were a child?"

Answer: "They ordered from the Sears Catalog. They made what they needed."

Question: "Can you tell me about one special thing that was really different from your childhood and mine?"

Answer: "They had no electricity or gas."

Unquestionably, Ruby Mae Etherton Owens has lived a long and full life. She has witnessed a great deal of change in her 90 plus years. When talking to Ruby about her past, she often declares with considerable pride, "I think I've done pretty good."

Yes, Ruby, Mrs. Owens, BeBe, Mother, Ma, Mom, Nana, Meme, Mammy, Aunt Ruby, you have in fact "done pretty good!"

Family Picture 2007
First row left to right: Abigale Samborski, Levi Samborski
Second row left to right: Amelia Samborski, Judy Leonard, Ruby Owens,
Rochelle Balkam, Tara Mathena
Third row left to right: Jennifer Samborski, Jane Owens, Robert Leonard
Fourth row left to right: David Samborski, James Owens